The Complete Handbook of Gardening Tips

by

Janet Macdonald

United Research Publishers

Published in the United States by United Research Publishers as *The Complete Handbook of Gardening Tips.*

ISBN 1-887053-10-7

Copyright © MCMXCV by Carnell Ltd.

Published in Great Britain by Carnell Ltd. as *The Complete Book of Gardening Tips.*

No part of this publication maybe transmitted or reproduced by any means whatsoever, whether electronic or mechanical, which includes photocopying, photographing, aural or written recording or stored in any form of retrieval apparatus without the written consent and permission of the publisher.

Book design by The Final Draft, Encinitas, CA

Cover design by The Art Department, Encinitas, CA

Order additional copies from:

    United Research Publishers
    P.O. Box 232344
    Encinitas, CA 92023-2344

90-day money back guarantee if not satisfied.

Preface

This book is unique in that it combines the best gardening tips, advice and shortcuts from both Britain and the United States.

Britain has long been known for its graceful and elegant gardens. These gardens are characterized by brilliant colors, incredible space utilization and overall breathtaking beauty. The United States is also known for its outstanding gardens and the cultivation of indoor plants from around the world. Gardening is the most popular leisure activity in the U.S. according to the National Gardening Association.

Section I of this book is the work of Janet Macdonald, a noted authority on gardening in Britain. She has been collecting gardening tips and shortcuts throughout her long and distinguished career and holds nothing back in covering what she has learned. The information in this section is applicable to North America as well as Britain.

Section II of this book contains valuable tips from Lorisa MW Mock. Lorisa has over 18 years of experience in both public and commercial horticulture. Lorisa interned and gardened at the world famous Longwood Gardens in Pennsylvania. She has presented research papers at a number of national conferences and has published numerous articles on gardening topics.

There is also a short glossary of unfamilar terms on page 233, to assist you in British/American translations.

Introduction

Gardening is the most popular leisure occupation in this country. It gives more pleasure to more people than any other activity—but at the same time it can also cause a lot of aching backs!

There is no denying that creating and maintaining a beautiful and productive garden does involve a fair amount of hard work. But where work has to be done, clever people always find short-cuts to get the job done quickly and easily.

I've been collecting short-cut tips throughout my gardening career and I've invented quite a few myself. They're all set down here for you to try, split into logical categories for easy reference.

Some are on design consideration, some on easing the task, some on saving money, and some are just plain fun—but they all work. I hope you find them as useful as I do.

Janet Macdonald

CONTENTS

Preface i
Introduction iii
Section I, Gardening Tips from Britain 1
    Acid soil and acid-loving plants 3
    Alpine plants and rock-gardens 3
    Annual flowers 5
    Autumn colour 6
    Beans and peas 8
    Beds and borders 9
    Birds in the garden 15
    Bonsai 18
    Bottle gardens and terraria 19
    Bulbs 21
    Buying plants 26
    Cacti and succulents 28
    Chalky or alkaline soil 29
    Children in the garden 31
    Chrysanthemums 32
    Clay soil 33
    Climbing plants 34
    Colour schemes 39
    Companion planting 40
    Compost making 41
    Container growing 43
    Cut flowers 47
    Cuttings 50
    Dahlias 51
    Design 52
    Digging 54
    Dry flowers 55
    Edible flowers 57
    Eggshells 59
    Evening gardens 60
    Fences 61
    Fertilisers 62

Foliage	63
Frost	65
Fruit	65
Fuchsias	70
Furniture	71
Gates	72
Geraniums and pelargoniums	74
Gifts	75
Grasses	75
Green ethics	77
Greenhouses and other glass protection	77
Green manure	80
Green vegetables	81
Ground cover	82
Hanging baskets	83
Health	85
Hedges	87
Hedge trimming	90
Herbs	92
Houseplants	96
Lawns	101
The magic words	105
Minimum maintenance gardens	105
Money from your garden	106
Mulching	110
Noise	111
Nuts	112
Onions and other edible allium	113
Open Day—letting the public into your garden	115
Orchids	116
Ornamental kitchen gardens	117
Paths and steps	119
Patios	120
Pests	121
Pets in the garden	123
Photographs	125
Ponds and other water features	127

Pot-pourri	131
Potting and other composts	132
Pressed flowers	133
Propagating	135
Pruning	139
Raised beds	140
Removing large trees	141
Root vegetables	142
Roses	144
Safety in the garden	146
Salad crops	148
Scented plants	150
Seaside gardens	152
Seeds	153
Selling your house?	158
Shady areas	159
Sheds	161
Shrubs	162
Sink gardens	163
Snow	164
Storing fruit and vegetables	164
Strawberries	166
Sweet corn	168
Sweet peas	170
Thinning	171
Tomatoes	172
Tools and equipment	174
Topiary	178
Traditional cottage gardens	179
Trees	180
Trellis	183
Tunnels and arches	183
Vegetables	184
Walls	186
Watering	188
Weeds	190
Wild flower gardens	192

Wildlife in the garden	193
Window-boxes	196
Wind protection	197
Winter colour	198
Zinnias and other odds and ends	198
Section II, Garden Tips from America	**203**
Advice	205
Annuals	205
Bulbs	206
Buying plants	207
Children in the garden (See also, Wildlife)	207
Chrysanthemums	208
Cut flowers	209
Design points	209
Digging	210
Dried flowers	210
Easy to grow plants	211
Evening gardens	211
Grasses	211
Health	212
Herbs	212
Houseplants	213
Labelling	215
Lawns	215
Mulch	216
Peonies	217
Pests of houseplants	217
Plant names	220
Staking	220
Tomatoes	221
Trees and shrubs	221
Wildlife and other pests	221
Winter	222
Extra Tips	**225**
Air Freshening Plants	227
Herbs	227
Vegetables	228

Water	230
Final words from "The Black Thumb"	230
Glossary	233
Index	235

Section I

Gardening Tips from Britain

Janet Macdonald has done a brilliant job in compiling a wealth of information on tips and shortcuts to make your gardening more pleasurable and less work. Some of the information presented in this section has impressed even some of the most accomplished gardening experts in the United States. Some of the comments have been: "why didn't I know about this"..."how did she ever learn such useful facts" ..."who is this lady and how does she know so much about gardening and plants."

Whether you're a seasoned gardener or just beginning, you will find this section highly informative and enjoyable to read. You'll soon be putting Janet's ideas to work for you and telling others some of the great things you have learned.

Acid soil and acid-loving plants

These are the easiest to grow and most popular acid-loving plants. Try them yourself: azaleas, camellia, rhododendron, heather, blueberries, Chilean flame flower, bearberry, kingcup, gentians, eucryphia.

❖ Test your soil with a testing kit before buying plants.

❖ If you live in a hard water area, save rainwater for your lime-hating plants.

❖ If your soil is sandy and free-draining as well as acid, add plenty of compost and mulches to aid water retention.

❖ For acid-loving plants in an alkaline-soiled garden, build a raised bed to fill with appropriate compost. If you don't want to use peat, use composted bark, coir, or coco shells.

❖ Try the acid-loving climber Chilean flame flower (*Tropaeolum speciosum*). It needs shade and moisture, but if it likes you it will cover your hedges and trees with brilliant scarlet flowers.

❖ Grow your own blueberries (*Vaccinium corymbosum*). They need a very acid soil, below pH 5.5, and plenty of moisture.

Alpine plants and rock-gardens

These are the easiest to grow and most popular alpine and rock-garden plants. Try them yourself: alyssum, anemone, aquilegia, arabis, campanula, glory of the snow, corydalis, broom, daphne, gentian, hardy geranium, iberis, juniper, potentilla, primula, pasque flower, dwarf willow, saxifraga, scilla, thyme, veronica.

- ❖ Use low walls with hollow tops to grow alpine plants such as saxifrages.

- ❖ Site rock-gardens in full sun and away from trees which will drop leaves onto the plants.

- ❖ Mix plenty of grit with the soil as most alpine plants require good drainage.

- ❖ For the most natural effect, lay the rocks so that the natural lines will run the same way, mimicking the strata in a real mountainside.

- ❖ Make a deep scree bed of stone chippings on the lowest level of your rock-garden. Use this for the plants which require the most drainage.

- ❖ Protect alpine plants from rain-induced winter rotting with a pane of glass laid over them. Support the glass on wooden pegs and weigh it down with a large stone.

- ❖ Use a terra cotta strawberry pot to grow saxifrages or sempervivums, choosing varieties with pink tinges to complement the colour of the pot.

- ❖ If your alpine mat-forming plants go bald in the middle, put a heavy stone in the centre of the plant and fill the spaces round it with compost to allow the plant to grow back in.

Alpine plants and rock-gardens

❖ Since many alpine plants are small, to appreciate them better, grow them in pots which can be kept up off the ground, closer to eye-level.

❖ If you can't afford to buy good sized rocks for a rock-garden, grow your alpines in a scree bed. This is basically a deep bed filled with granite chippings, with some larger stones strategically placed to give a natural effect. Choose plants that are all of the same scale.

❖ Make a miniature alpine garden in an old stone sink. To give it some height, include a dwarf conifer, or a chunk of tufa which stands above the surface and can have planting holes made in it.

❖ When buying alpine plants, check that they haven't started to rot at the base by brushing your hand across them. If they lift off the compost, leave them.

❖ When building a rock-garden, use a local stone to blend in with the other surroundings.

Annual flowers

These are the easiest to grow and most popular annual plants. Try them yourself: ageratum, alyssum, antirrhinum, calendula, centaurea, clarkia, cosmos, larkspur, pinks, godetia, gypsophila, helichrysum, impatiens, linaria, lobelia, nasturtium, nemesia, nicotiana, phlox, poppy, salvia, stock, sweet pea, tagetes, verbena, viola, zinnia.

- ❖ Wait until all risk of frost is past before you buy summer bedding plants, unless you can keep them under cover. Plant them out when you see your town parks department put theirs out.

- ❖ If using the same bed for spring and summer displays, dig in compost before the autumn planting and apply a granular fertiliser after removing the spring plants.

- ❖ For patterns of different coloured flowers, mark where each type of plant is to go by outlining the area with a trail of sand.

- ❖ When buying summer bedding plants, choose the bushy ones which aren't yet in flower.

- ❖ Use annuals to fill in the gaps in your new perennial plantings.

- ❖ Get your annual climbers such as sweet peas, nasturtiums or black-eyed Susan (*Thunbergia alata*) off to a good start indoors, then set out their supports before you add the plants.

Autumn colour

These are the easiest to grow and most popular autumn colour plants. Try them yourself: grape vine, heather, larch, liquidambar, maple, poplar, prunus, sumach, Turkey oak, Virginia creeper, witch hazel.

- ❖ Site your autumn colour trees and shrubs where they will be protected from gales and early frosts.

- Make sure autumn flowering perennials are well staked to keep them upright in autumn winds.

- Colour-theme your autumn foliage display by choosing trees and shrubs with either red and purple, orange and bronze or yellow and brown leaf colours.

- Consider the Sorbus group of trees, for various leaf and berry colour. For instance, 'Joseph Rock' has yellow berries and 'November Pink' has pink berries.

- Fill in the spaces in front of your autumn colour shrubs with sedums and autumn flowering bulbs such as nerines and colchicums for some low level colour.

- For unusual colour in your tubs and window-boxes, try the ornamental cabbages and kales. They are easy to grow and develop their full colour as the weather gets colder.

- Grow Japanese maples in oriental-style pots on your patio to bring their attractive leaves close to the house.

- To get a good display of berries on firethorn (*Pyracantha*), be sparing when you prune it. Choose from varieties with berries ranging from yellow to orangey-red, and upright or spreading habits.

- Choose varieties of Michaelmas daisies that are mildew resistant. Split the clumps every other year to keep a good supply of flowers coming.

Beans and peas

❖ Ignore people who tell you to sow peas at carefully spaced intervals. Sow them thickly in wide trenches and they will need little support as the plants will help hold each other up. Choose one of the semi-leafless varieties like Bikini and they will need no support.

❖ When creating poles to support runner beans or ornamental climbers put a rubber band over each pole. As the plant grows, move the band up the pole.

❖ To get an early crop of peas, start them in the greenhouse in a length of guttering or folded strips of polythene. When the peas are 3" (8cm) tall and have plenty of root, take out a shallow trench, lay the gutter or polythene strips in the trench and slide them out from under the pea plants. To make this easier, lay a couple of lengths of binder twine in the bottom before putting in the compost. Knot them together at the ends, and hook them over a short stick stuck in the ground before pulling away the guttering.

❖ Grow white-flowered and white-seeded runner beans such as 'The Czar' and let some mature completely. Shell the beans out of the pod, dry them and use them instead of butter-beans.

❖ Runner beans need plenty of water to produce a good crop, so make a trench between the rows before erecting your canes, and just pour water into this trench instead of watering each plant.

❖ Prevent mice from stealing your newly sown pea seeds by sprinkling slug pellets, paraffin, or some other strongly scented material, on the soil. It's the smell of germinating peas that attracts the mice, and the other strong scents disguise the scent of peas.

❖ Pick peas and beans as soon as they are big enough to eat. All the time you keep picking, the plant will produce more, but if you let them mature the plant thinks it has done its job and stops production.

❖ When erecting canes for runner beans, cross them half-way up rather than near the top, so the beans hang outside for easier picking.

❖ To straighten out runner beans for the show bench, pick them and roll them up in damp cloth for at least 12 hours. They will be pliable enough to gently straighten them, then tie them up in a damp cloth again with a straight piece of wood to keep them in shape.

Beds and borders

These are the easiest to grow and most popular bedding plants. Try them yourself: ageratum, antirrhinum, begonia, daisy, calceolaria, campanula, coleus, cosmos, dahlia, dianthus, impatiens, myosotis, nemesia, nicotiana, pelargonium, penstemon, petunia, phlox, primula, salvia, scabiosa, sweet William, tagetes, verbena, viola, wallflower, zinnia.

❖ Plant perennials in groups of three, then, when the plants need splitting, take up one, split it and put the resulting smaller plants into pots to grow on. The following year, you'll have good plants ready to take over from the others, and won't have bald patches in your border.

❖ Split Michaelmas daisies every two years for good quality flower spikes and better resistance to mildew.

❖ Add decorative vegetables to your bedding schemes. Red or white stemmed chard, curly-leaved parsley, beetroot, red cabbage, asparagus or the wonderful green fountains of sweet corn are every bit as attractive as many of the more expensive ornamental plants.

❖ To gain the tropical effect of canna lilies without the expense and time involved, buy some tropical tubers such as yams from the vegetable section of your supermarket and pot these up. Give them some bottom heat and they will soon put out shiny leaves on long stems. Plant them out when all danger of frost is past.

❖ Check your border carnations after frost in case they have been pushed up out of the soil, and firm them back in carefully.

❖ For the best results with border carnations, buy young plants in pots from a specialist grower. Increase your stock from established plants by layering basal shoots or taking cuttings just below a node.

❖ For a sequence of flowers over a long period, choose day lilies (*Hemerocallis*). Colours range from cream through orange to deep red, and the plants are long-lived.

❖ Buy one foxglove plant, put it at the back of a border or in a shady spot and let it seed. You will then have foxgloves for as long as you want.

❖ To select out common purple foxgloves from whites and other colours, check the seedlings as soon as they have real leaves and remove the ones with purple tinges on the leaf stalks.

❖ Try some of the less common irises for a longer display of flowers than given by bearded irises. *Iris siberica* forms large clumps and will tolerate some shade, while *Iris kaempferi* with its mixed colour flowers will give you colour in July and August. This one prefers damp places.

❖ For really satisfactory wallflowers and sweet Williams, grow them yourself from seed, then move them into 3" (8cm) pots or space them out in a nursery bed so they can form really strong, bushy plants before you move them to their final place in the autumn.

- If you like plants that sprawl over the edge of their bed, such as lady's mantle *(Alchemilla mollis)* locate them next to a path rather than a lawn, which will suffer from being smothered.

- Grow lupins as biennials to enjoy their brief flowering period without having their space cluttered for the rest of the year. Sow the seeds in pots in April, plant them out in autumn, and consign them to the compost heap after flowering. Replace them with something that flowers later on, like dahlias or asters.

- If you do leave lupins in place, put something that will spread sideways next to them, and cut the lupins down to the ground after flowering.

- For the best lupins, restrict each plant to four flower spikes. Sever the other shoots at the base of the plant, preferably with some rootstock attached, and use these as cuttings.

- To keep the leaves of the grey foliage plant *Senecio ceucostachys* as pale as possible, you have to restrict the roots, so put them into your borders in their pots.

- For a spring display of bulbs and biennials such as wallflowers or sweet Williams, plant them in September to allow the plants to become established before hard frosts.

- When planting for a spring display, put the bulbs in last. Otherwise you may leave gaps by put-

Beds and borders

ting a plant in on top of a bulb. This could also damage the bulb.

❖ Divide your bearded irises every three years to keep the flowers coming.

❖ Divide clumps of bamboo in June, preferably on a damp day so the roots won't dry out. Each new clump should have two or three canes, which you can cut down to about 12" (30cm) for easier handling.

❖ Peonies prefer not to be moved, but if you must move them, prepare the new planting hole before digging the plant up, as this reduces the risk of the feeder roots drying up. Make sure the new site is well-drained.

❖ Give alstromerias a good start by protecting their roots with mulch or fleece during their first two winters. They should be in a sheltered, sunny position where they will not be disturbed.

❖ Grow the white-striped grass gardeners garters (*Phalaris arundinacea*) next to the feathery foliage of bronze fennel (*Foeniculum vulgare* 'Purpurescens'). Each will show off the other by providing a contrast of texture as well as colour.

❖ When planting out container-grown plants, gently tease out any roots which have curled round the bottom of the pot. This encourages them to spread their roots quickly into the soil.

- Wait until early spring to tidy up your perennial beds and borders. If you do it in the autumn, you will miss the decorative effect of hoar frost on seed-heads, deprive birds of the seeds, and deprive your plants of the protection their dead stems and foliage give from severe weather.

- Enjoy the variegated leaves of *Iris pallida* 'Variegata' by planting it at the front of a border. Pink candelabra primulas go well with it.

- Plant a selection of kniphofia to get flowers from May to October.

- Take advantage of the dry conditions at the bottom of a south facing wall to make a Mediterranean garden. With some shelter from the wind, the wall will act like a storage heater to provide the right conditions for tender plants such as the unusual French lavender (*Lavandula stoechas*).

- Amuse your guests on summer evenings by growing burning bush (*Dictamnus albus*) and applying a lighted match just above the flowers. The volatile oils they give off will ignite and flare.

- Put sharp sand round your hostas and spring bulbs. This will discourage slugs and show you where the plants are in the winter.

- Provide support for all your border plants in one operation by putting stakes at each corner of the border to stand 2' (60cm) high, then attach a roll of wide mesh netting over the whole border for the plants to grow through.

❖ Choose modern hybrid border pinks if you want a long flowering season from them—the old-fashioned varieties only flower once a year.

❖ Make your own supports for perennial border plants with five or six canes and some string. As soon as the plant has started growing in the spring, push the canes into the soil round the outside of the plant and tie the string round and across the canes to make a 'cat's cradle' support for the tall growth.

Birds in the garden

❖ Leave old swallows' nests in place. The swallows will use them again next year, and they provide winter shelter for wrens.

❖ Wrens are too shy to come to bird tables, so put food for them under shrubs. They like finely grated cheese or wholemeal breadcrumbs.

❖ Put out a mixture of food to provide for different birds. Robins like finely chopped suet or cheese and thrushes like oatmeal while other birds like sliced apples, peanuts and raisins as well as seeds and grains.

❖ Check the water in your birdbath every day and keep it topped up in summer and unfrozen in winter. Birds get used to a daily bath and will abandon a birdbath that is only erratically available.

- When topping up bird water in winter, throw away any ice that has formed and replace it with warm water. This is much quicker and easier than adding boiled water to ice.

- Buy only peanuts that are British Standards Association marked for bird feeding or human consumption. There is a danger that unmarked nuts could be contaminated by a poisonous mould.

- Stop putting out peanuts at the end of April as tits may feed them whole to their babies who could choke on them.

- Attach empty half coconut shells to beams in sheds and outhouses to encourage robins or swallows to nest.

- Make a simple and cheap birdbath from a dustbin-lid sunk into the soil or propped up on bricks.

- Make a simple but ornamental birdbath with a clay pot saucer fitted into the top of an old chimneypot.

- Buy or make birdbaths that can be moved from shade in summer to a sunny, sheltered place in the winter.

- To stop the squirrels stealing the nuts you put out for the birds, hang the nuts on a cane smeared with car grease.

Birds in the garden

❖ Remember that birds need water in the winter as well as in the summer.

❖ Put bird food out at the same time every day. You'll soon find the birds are waiting for you. If you go on holiday in the winter, get a neighbour to feed them at the same time.

❖ Grow giant sunflowers for seed-eating birds. Cut the heads off as they ripen and hang them up where the birds will find them.

❖ Help thrushes to rid your garden of snails by providing them with a large stone to use as an anvil for breaking the shells.

❖ Attract birds to your garden by growing berry-bearing trees and shrubs such as holly, hawthorn, cotoneaster, pyracantha and snowberry.

❖ Use empty wire peanut tubes to supply nesting material in spring. Fill them with pieces of wool, combings from your dog or even human hair—all will be welcome.

❖ Encourage those wonderful insect eaters, blue tits into your garden by making nest-boxes for them, but make sure the hole is no bigger than 1" (3cm) in diameter. Any bigger and sparrows will take over and evict the blue tits.

❖ Use 8-10" (20-25cm) clay flower pots as nesting-boxes. Chip out the bottom hole a little, then attach them to a tree or shed with wire and galvanized nails.

- ❖ Keep an old mug near your cooker and fill it with spare fat, then hang it up for the blue tits.

- ❖ Roll out spare bits of pastry, press bird seed into them, and wrap them round string before baking them and hanging them up for the birds.

- ❖ Build an aviary to keep more exotic birds in your garden. The style should fit in with the surroundings, the whole thing should be rat-proof: and the inside should be bird-proof as even budgerigars will destroy wood in a surprisingly short time.

Bonsai

- ❖ For the best drainage, use a basic potting mixture of equal parts of peat, loam, and sharp sand.

- ❖ For pines and junipers, use a compost which is 70 per cent sharp sand, 15 per cent peat and 15 per cent loam.

- ❖ For azaleas and rhododendrons, use up to 50 per cent peat in the compost.

- ❖ Apply fertilisers only in the growing season. From early spring to mid-summer give high nitrogen mixes, from mid-summer to early autumn, give low nitrogen mixes.

- ❖ Water your bonsai every evening in the growing season, and every morning as well in hot summer weather. Only water in the dormant season if the compost is completely dry.

- ❖ To create your own bonsai subjects, try air-layering branches from mature trees. This is especially effective with flowering subjects like wisteria.

- ❖ Use a power router to remove strips of bark and create the prized 'driftwood' effect on trunk and branches. Alternatively, train a live sapling round a dead branch.

- ❖ Train branches and trunk into shape with heavy copper or aluminium wire.

- ❖ To give the effect of a tree clinging to a rock, glue lengths of wire to the rock with epoxy resin and use these wires to hold the roots in place.

- ❖ Avoid pots which are glazed inside, as this adversely affects drainage.

- ❖ If you bring your bonsai into the house, keep them moist by misting them with water every day.

Bottle gardens and terraria

- ❖ Choose clear glass bottles, as plants don't thrive in the green glass versions.

- ❖ Save money by making your own terrarium from a kit.

- ❖ For a simple, ready-made terrarium, use an old fish bowl or tank.

- ❖ Make sure your chosen container has plenty of height, or your plants will look cramped.

- If your fancy is for tropical plants that need heat, use a plant propagator with high sides, a domed lid, and a thermostatic temperature control.

- As a cheaper alternative to an acid carboy, use a glass sweet jar.

- Use soilless potting compost mixed with a little charcoal to prevent algae building up.

- To prevent overcrowding, choose small plants which are slow growing or easy to prune. Good garden centres will label them suitable for bottle gardens.

- Look for plants with interestingly shaped and coloured leaves.

- Avoid flowering plants for small-necked bottle gardens: it is difficult to remove the dead flowers.

- Before installing your new plants, soak them in water to thoroughly wet the compost; remove some of the surface compost to reduce the risk of introducing algae and weeds to your container.

- Make up a set of tools on bamboo canes to reach inside tall bottles—a razor-blade for pruning, a needle for picking up prunings, a cotton reel for tamping compost, a teaspoon for digging, a sponge to clean the glass inside.

- Water by inserting a pipe down to compost level and trickling water in, not by pouring it through the neck of the bottle as this could wash the compost away from the plants.

- ❖ Make a miniature Japanese garden in a fish tank with some interesting stones, raked sand, and a bonsai tree.

Bulbs

These are the easiest to grow and most popular bulbs. Try them yourself: acidanthera, allium, alstromeria, begonia, chionodoxa, crocus, freesia, fritillary, gladiolus, grape hyacinth, hyacinth, narcissus species, snowdrop, tulip.

- ❖ Buy the biggest tulip bulbs available. The bigger the bulb, the more years they will flower without your having to fuss over them.

- ❖ Buy large quantities of bulbs to get a discount and share them with friends.

- ❖ Layer bulbs in containers to get a longer display; for instance, tulips halfway down the container with narcissus and crocuses on top.

- ❖ For successful flowering, plant crown imperials (*Fritilleria imperialis*) in a well-drained place in full sun. They dislike damp places.

- ❖ Plant daffodils at least 6" (15cm) deep to prevent them from drying up in hot summers.

- ❖ For a long-lasting display of bright pinks and reds, choose the early double tulips. They look stunning in a hanging basket with primulas and pansies.

- Plant lily bulbs on a mound of grit to prevent the water-logging they hate, and work more grit into the soil around them.

- Most of the ornamental alliums have scruffy leaves, so hide these with annuals such as nigella.

- Remove a slab from your patio in the autumn and plant bulbs, adding a layer of gravel to the surface. The slab can be replaced in summer when the bulbs have died down. Choose bulbs that will contrast with the surrounding slabs, such as white narcissus with pink slabs or blue hyacinths with grey.

- Create a white spring display by combining white tulips, narcissus, grape hyacinths and fritillaries (*Fritillaria meleagris*) 'Alba' or 'Aphrodite,' white forget-me-nots, lily of the valley and a white variegated hosta. For an earlier display, plant snowdrops in front of a white-flowered hellebore (*H. orientalis*).

- To get away from the same old spring bulbs that all your neighbours grow, try dogs tooth violets (*Erythronium denscanis*), or camassia (*C. leichtlinii*) which has 3' (1m) high flower spikes in blue or white.

- Prepare your own bulbs for early flowering the same way commercial growers do, by making the bulb believe it has gone through a whole year since flowering. Once the leaves have died back, lift and dry the bulbs. Keep them in a hot place for several weeks to mimic summer, then in the refrigerator for a few weeks to mimic winter, before bringing them back into the warm and potting them up as usual.

❖ Plant bulbs under other plants whose growing leaves will hide the unsightly foliage of the bulbs after flowering.

❖ Plant the foxtail lily (*Eremurus elwesii*) on a large stone or piece of slate to prevent it water-logging and rotting.

❖ Use plastic net orange bags to heel-in bulbs when they have finished flowering. Tie a label to the bag and leave the handles above the soil. When the leaves have died back, just pull the bag out of the ground, give it a shake to get rid of the soil and hang it up to dry the bulbs out.

❖ Deadhead all your bulbs after flowering to prevent them putting energy into producing seeds when they should be putting it back into the bulbs for next year's flowers.

❖ Use a horse whip or hazel switch to deadhead your bulbs without having to bend.

❖ Provide support for tall hyacinths by pushing the stick through the bulb. As long as you don't damage the flower stem, this will not hurt the bulb.

❖ To stop squirrels digging up your bulbs, cover the planted areas with wire netting. If you don't like the look of it, cover the netting with a thin layer of soil. The bulbs will grow through it, or you can take it up when the leaves show.

❖ Keep an eye on your stored bulbs, corms and tubers during the winter and remove any that show signs of disease or rot before it spreads to the others.

❖ There is no need to lift tulip bulbs from borders. Leave them in place and they will gradually increase. Do mark their location with some short sticks so you don't accidentally dig them up later in the year.

❖ Plant tulips among your bearded irises. They will work their way up between the iris rhizomes quite happily.

❖ Don't pay a fortune for the tall lilac pompons of *Allium gigantium* when leek flowers are just as tall and every bit as decorative. The price of one Allium bulb will buy you many packets of leek seed.

❖ For a splash of pink in the autumn, try the Jersey lily (*Nerine bowdenii*). Leave them in place and they will increase quickly. They like to be planted with their necks above the soil, and will push their way up if you put them in too deep.

❖ For keen flower arrangers as well as gardeners, try the giant headed *Allium christophii*. This is the one that forms a 10" (25cm) ball of star-like flowers that hold their shape when dry. The flower-heads stand 18-24" (45-60cm) above the ground, which gives you room for something else underneath.

❖ If planting daffodils to naturalise under trees, choose the smaller flowered species which look better in this setting than modern big-flowered hybrids. Groups of one type look better than random mixtures.

❖ For the most natural looking effect when planting bulbs under trees or in grass, throw the bulbs onto the ground in handfuls and plant each one where it lands. This avoids the artificial look of even spacing.

❖ Rather than the usual arrangement of tulips spaced out between wallflowers or forget-me-nots, try a clump of tulips on their own at the back.

❖ Transplant snowdrops and winter aconites 'in the green,' while they still have their leaves. They hate being moved as dry bulbs and will sulk or die on you.

❖ Buy bulbs by mail order, or as soon as they appear in the shops. They should be kept in cool conditions and will deteriorate while they sit on the shop shelves in the warm. Pick the firmest, with outer skin intact, and no blemishes.

❖ After flowering, remove the dead flower-heads then wait for six to eight weeks before removing the leaves. This allows the plant to complete its growing cycle and return nutrients to the bulb for next year's flowers. It is best not to tie daffodil leaves in knots.

❖ If established clumps of bulbs fail to flower, feed them with a liquid fertiliser, wait for the leaves to die down, then lift and divide the clumps before replanting them.

❖ To plant groups of small bulbs in grass, lift a strip of turf and loosen the soil with a fork before planting the bulbs and replacing the turf.

❖ For easy lifting and storing of bulbs, place a plastic mesh bowl in the ground and plant the bulbs inside it. Then, when the flowers and foliage have died back, lift the whole bowl with its contents for storage.

❖ To enjoy flowering bulbs in summer as well as spring, try planting pineapple flowers (*Eucomis comosa*), alliums, gladioli, camassia (*C. quamash*) or freesia.

❖ Keep lilies and 'broken coloured' tulips well separated. The virus that creates the colour effects in the tulips will kill the lilies.

Buying plants

❖ Before buying plants, check whether they require more time and attention to be spent on them than you are prepared to give. If you have a busy lifestyle, you may not want plants that have to be staked, mulched, deadheaded, pruned, divided, fertilised, sprayed against pests and diseases and constantly watered, especially if another similar plant needs none of this fuss.

❖ Before you buy any herbaceous perennial, find out how long it flowers for. If they are only in flower for a couple of weeks, and have neither attractive leaves nor berries, you may decide they are not worth the space they will take up. Many gardeners feel this way about bearded irises and lupins.

❖ Buy unusual plants when you go garden visiting. Many gardens which are open to the public, especially those organised through the National Gardens Scheme, frequently have examples of the plants they grow for sale at reasonable prices.

❖ Make sure plants sold in containers have been grown in the containers, not just recently planted in them. The soil should be firm and the whole mass of soil and roots should lift out of the container easily.

❖ Always subject plants to a close inspection for pests. Even if you intend to keep the plant in its container for a while, lift it out of the container to check for grubs or eggs underneath.

❖ When plants arrive by post, give them a drink straight away and keep them moist until you are ready to plant them.

- ❖ When buying bedding plants, choose short, compact plants which are ready to grow on strongly rather than tall, spindly plants which may have been forced into growth and will take a long time to recover.
- ❖ If you live near London and need a lot of bedding plants, get up early and go to New Covent Garden market. It'll cost you a few pounds to get in, but your plants will cost a fraction of the retail price.
- ❖ Check out the named varieties of your favourite plants and insist on the variety that has the qualities you want. Other varieties may be disappointing.

Cacti and succulents

- ❖ *Don't put cacti on chairs!*
- ❖ Keep dormant cacti dry in winter to prevent basal rotting.
- ❖ Let cacti and succulents dry out completely between waterings. Water frequently in spring and summer to encourage flowering.
- ❖ Repot cacti in late winter, but only if they are obviously too big for their pots. Use a specialist compost.
- ❖ To protect your hands when repotting cacti, fold a couple of sheets of newspaper into a strip to wrap round the plant.

- Keep an eye out for mealy bugs, which hide in wool-like patches at the base of the plant. Dab methylated spirits on them, using a cotton bud or artists paintbrush.

- Leave Christmas cacti (*Schlumbergera*) in the same place once they have formed flowerbuds. If you have to move the pot to dust, mark it and put it back in exactly the right place or it will drop its buds.

- Use cacti and succulents in window-boxes and hanging baskets for an unusual summer display.

- **Knit your own cacti from pale green angora wool.** Pot them up like real ones and nobody will know unless they get really close.

Chalky or alkaline soil

- The only plants you can't grow in chalky soil are those listed under 'acid-loving plants.' Have fun and try them all!

- If in doubt about the degree of chalkiness in your soil, use a soil testing kit. Colour comparison kits are cheaper and easier to use than 'poke in the ground' meters.

- Don't let people who like rhododendrons and heather tell you that you won't make a decent garden on chalky soil—it's not true. You just have to choose your plants carefully.

❖ Create a rock-garden with the alpine plants which like chalk, including aubretia, miniature dianthus and creeping thymes.

❖ Growing beans, potatoes and tomatoes can be difficult on chalky soil, so use plenty of manure or compost. This can be more easily done where the soil is shallow as well as chalky by making a raised bed to confine the compost. Add spent growbag compost to these beds.

❖ If you can't live without lime-hating plants, make a raised peat bed, or dig a hole, line it with a thick butyl pond-liner, and fill it with acid soil. Don't forget drainage holes.

❖ Visit chalk-land gardens which are open to the public to see what they are growing. Take a notebook to list species and varieties that catch your eye.

❖ Chalky soils often lack nutrients, so use lots of manure and compost.

❖ Choose from climbers which like chalky soil such as clematis, ivy and honeysuckle.

❖ Choose from trees which like or tolerate chalky soil. These include maples (*Acer*), horse chestnut, birch, Judas tree (*Cercis siliquastrum*), hawthorns, spindleberry (*Euonymus europaeus*), laburnum, mountain ash (*Sorbus aucuparia*).

❖ Choose from shrubs which like or tolerate chalky

soil. These include bamboos, spotted laurel (*Aucuba japonica*), berberis, buddleia, japonica (*Chaenomeles*), cotoneaster, smoke bush (*Cotinus coggygria*), daphne, hibiscus, broom, lilac, magnolia, mock orange (*Philadelphus*), roses and viburnum.

Children in the garden

❖ Cover ponds with stout netting to prevent small children falling in, or convert the pond into a sand pit until the children are older.

❖ Anchor large play equipment, such as climbing frames or swings, firmly to the ground so that it will not tip over when abused by rough children.

❖ Encourage children to take an interest in the garden by growing things which put on rapid growth, such as the herbs lovage or angelica which both shoot up their flower spikes at over 6" (15cm) a day.

❖ Amuse children by giving them a Halloween pumpkin with their name on. Write the name on the tender young fruits as soon as they are big enough to write on, applying just enough pressure to bruise the skin, and the name will grow as the pumpkin does.

❖ Encourage young children to grow things by helping them to write their name in the soil with a stick, then sowing fast germinating seeds such as pot marigolds so they can see their name in plants.

❖ For a family garden, choose hard-wearing grasses for a lawn, avoid hard surfaces or sharp edges where a toddler might fall, and put soft surfaces such as shredded bark under swings or climbing frames.

❖ Cover sand pits when not in use to prevent cats fouling them.

Chrysanthemums

❖ Recycle potted chrysanthemums into garden plants by snipping off the dead flower-heads and separating the plants before planting them out 18" (45cm) apart. Give them a feed to help them recover from the dwarfing chemicals they have been sprayed with, and let them grow on to flower naturally in the autumn.

❖ Choose hardy varieties to grow outside, and cover the roots with a layer of straw or bracken to help them get through the winter. Divide the clumps every three years to keep them vigorous.

❖ To create bushy plants for the border, nip out the growing tips of the main shoots.

❖ To raise good sized flowers for cutting, nip out the main growing tip to encourage side shoots, then remove all side buds to leave one main bud.

Stake the plants and support individual flower stems with canes.

❖ **Grow bedding chrysanthemums upside down** in a hanging basket. Buy or grow rooted cuttings in 3" (8cm) square pots—you'll need about 30 plants for an average sized basket. In early July, insert all but nine of the plants into the sides of the basket in the usual way, then fill nine empty 3" (8cm) square pots with compost only and pack these into the top of the basket. Put a large board over the top of the basket and turn it upside down, leaving it like this for about four weeks until the plants have covered the basket. Then turn it the right way up, exchange the nine empty pots for the last nine plants, and hang the basket in the usual way. All the plants will now grow upwards and by the autumn you will have an impressive display of flowers.

Clay soil

❖ Do your main digging tasks in the autumn when the soil will be moist enough to dig without being so claggy you can't move it.

❖ Dig shallowly to avoid bringing up the even clayier sub-soil which will spoil the top-soil you do have.

❖ Buy a load of medium fine grit from a builders' merchant and add one barrowload to each square yard of soil. Do this once a year.

- ❖ Top-dress your lawn with fine grit each autumn, at the rate of one bucketful per square yard (metre).

- ❖ Add a generous sprinkle of lime whenever you dig, unless you intend to grow potatoes on a particular patch. Alternatively, use horticultural gypsum.

- ❖ Add as much organic matter as you can get hold of.

- ❖ Keep your borders and beds narrow enough so that you do not have to walk on them when cultivating. Alternatively, buy or make some stepping stones to avoid compacting the soil by walking on it.

- ❖ Build deep beds to create deeper layers of soil, especially if you want to grow vegetables. Use old railway sleepers or scaffold boards for the bed edges.

- ❖ Put cloches or plastic sheeting over the areas you want to dig in the spring, especially in the vegetable garden, as this will give the soil a chance to dry out before you work it.

Climbing plants

These are the easiest to grow and most popular climbers. Try them yourself: actinidia, clematis, eccremocarpus, grape vine, honeysuckle, ivy, jasmin, nasturtium, passion flower, pyracantha, rose, solanum, tassle bush, wisteria.

❖ Try the Solanum family for climbers with decorative foliage, attractive berries and flowers in a range of colours from purple to white.

❖ To encourage wisteria to climb a tree, plant it away from the trunk, on the drip-line at the outer edge of the branches, then give it a chain or rope to guide it up into the tree. Anchor the chain to the ground with a strong peg, and leave it loose enough to allow for the movement of the tree on a windy day, or the wisteria could be pulled out of the ground.

❖ Be patient with clematis. It can take them a couple of years to establish a good root system before they put on a lot of top growth and start flowering prolifically.

❖ Grow a passion flower (*Passiflora spp.*) through a hedge to set off the flowers more attractively than its own foliage does. For the best effect combine the passion flower with golden privet, golden lonicera, or a golden conifer.

❖ Although it is not strictly a climber, train the common nasturtium (*Tropaeolum majus*) up supports or encourage it to scramble up a shrub or small tree and cheer things up with its bright flowers.

❖ Grow clematis so they creep through low shrubs, instead of making them climb. This is particularly effective with the varieties whose flowers face upwards.

❖ For an unusual flowering summer climber, try the tuberous nasturtium (*Tropaeolum tuberosum* 'Ken Aslet'). Grow it in pots indoors until all danger of frost is past, then take it outdoors and give it a thin cane to climb. The adventurous cook will be interested to know that the tubers are edible, and can be cooked like potatoes.

❖ Create a scented arbour with trellis and honeysuckle, clematis, wisteria or climbing roses.

❖ Provide a separate support system for plants grown against a pebble-dashed wall, or there is a risk that the weight of the plants will pull off sheets of pebble-dash.

❖ Use wire twist-ties for training plants to their supports. This is much quicker and less fiddly than using string.

❖ **Beg some telephone cable from your friendly neighbourhood telephone engineer**. This cable is made up of several strands of fine wire covered in plastic, which is the ideal plant tie.

❖ Keep an eye on the soil at the bottom of walls and water if necessary. The area close to walls tends to be very dry as rain doesn't reach it and the reflected heat of the wall also dries it out.

❖ Hide ugly dead trees or boring shrubs by growing flowering climbers up through them.

❖ If growing climbers against a wall that has to be painted at intervals, train them onto trellis that is mounted with hinges at the bottom and butterfly fasteners at the top edge.

❖ Check how your favourite climbing plants actually climb before providing support for them. The ones which cling on with tendrils, like passion flowers or sweet peas need fine wire or netting supports, while the ones which twine, like honeysuckle or hops will be happy with thicker supports like trellis.

❖ Try the golden hop (*Humulus lupulus* 'Aureus') to brighten a dull corner or cover an unsightly shed. It dies back in winter but will climb to over 10' (3m) each season. The colouring of its leaves makes them look as though someone had painted them for a 3-D effect, and its flowers give off a delightful soothing scent in late summer.

❖ Grow morning glory (*Ipomoea spp.*) only if you will be around in the mornings to enjoy their flowers. They need a sunny, east- or south-facing wall to do their best, but each individual flower only lasts a few hours.

❖ Runner beans have attractive flowers and can be grown as ornamentals. Choose the old variety 'Painted Lady' for its two tone pink and white flowers, or the Italian birled bean 'Tongues of Fire' for its yellow and red striped pods.

❖ For a north-facing wall, try the climbing *Hydrangea petiolaris*, but be prepared to wait two or three years for it to become established before it flowers.

- Plant a selection of honeysuckles to prolong the flowering season. Each variety flowers for several weeks, and if you choose a selection of varieties, you could have flowers from May to October. Be aware that not all varieties are scented.

- Use galvanised pig-wire rather than plastic netting to support climbing plants. The pig-wire is stronger than plastic and less obtrusive.

- Attach non-twining climbers such as roses to their support by tying them to the outside of the support, not by poking the growing tips through the mesh. Tying them makes pruning easy, poking them through makes pruning almost impossible.

- If planting a climber to cover an old tree, give it something to help it up the trunk, such as netting or bamboo canes. Plant the climber at least 18" (45cm) from the tree so you won't lose it if the tree has to go.

- When planting clematis from a container, don't try to tease out the roots as these can be brittle and break easily. Instead dig a large enough hole to add plenty of compost and bonemeal and plant with the root ball 3" (8cm) below the soil surface.

- Young clematis shoots are tender and tempting to slugs, so protect newly planted specimens with plenty of slug pellets or a short piece of plastic pipe.

❖ Use a circular washing line as a support for a flowering climber to create an attractive 'standard.'

Colour schemes

❖ Consider leaf colour as well as flower colour when planning a single coloured planting scheme.

❖ Keep your colour theme going by choosing plants which flower at different times.

❖ Try a 'traffic light' bed, with red at the back, yellow in the middle and green in the front. You could even do this in the vegetable garden with beetroot, swiss chard and red lettuces; yellow tomatoes, golden courgettes and onions; and any of the green leaf vegetables.

❖ Try a 'rainbow' bed, with all the colours of the rainbow in their proper sequence. In case you've forgotten what they are: red, orange, yellow, green, blue, indigo, violet.

❖ Accentuate your chosen colour with a few examples of another complementary colour. For instance, blue looks bluer with a little yellow.

❖ Carry your colour scheme through to your window-boxes and hanging baskets.

Companion planting

❖ Consider the cultural needs of different types of plants before locating them close together. The needs of one may be contraindicated for the other and your money and efforts will be wasted.

❖ **Grow garlic under roses to make the roses smell sweeter.**

❖ Grow onions and carrots together. The smell of onions confuses the carrot flies and the smell of carrots confuses the onion flies.

❖ Don't grow onions close to beans. The beans don't like it.

❖ Do grow celery next to beans for a bumper crop of beans.

❖ Plant French marigolds (*Tagetes*) with cabbages to discourage whitefly.

❖ **Always plant one petunia in each bed of onions.** The onions like it because it reminds them of the song!

❖ Plant pot marigolds (*Calendula*), nasturtiums, feverfew or borage close to anything that suffers from blackfly. The blackfly prefer these herbs and will leave the other plants alone.

❖ Grow beans in with your sweet corn. Beans fix nitrogen from the air in their root nodules and sweet corn loves nitrogen.

❖ Grow anise close to your brassicas. Its strong smell disguises the smell of the brassicas and confuses pests that detect cabbages by scent.

Compost making

❖ For fast compost production, wait until the first heat has died down, then turn the heap into another pile, remixing the contents and turning it sides-to-middle as you go.

❖ **Encourage your heap to heat up by adding what the Henry Doubleday Research Association coyly calls 'liquid household activator'— that's urine to the rest of us.**

❖ Make compost quicker by shredding everything before you put it into the compost heap. Small, even-sized pieces of material will heat up quicker.

❖ Don't put leather in your compost heap. Chromium salts used in the tanning process can build up in the soil, creating a toxic residue which reduces plant health—and if used on vegetable beds, could affect people who eat the produce.

❖ For a quickly constructed compost bin, nail four identically sized builders' pallets together to form a square.

❖ Don't waste your money on sectional plastic compost bins. They don't work any better than wooden or wire netting bins, and they tend to fall apart in a couple of seasons.

- ❖ Convert turfs into loam. Just stack them upside down somewhere they can stay for 12-18 months.

- ❖ Make leaf-mould in black plastic bags for a faster result than the traditional wire netting enclosure. Cram the bags full of leaves, tie the top and push it down to form a hollow that will catch rainwater. Punch a few holes to let the water in to the leaves, and leave it until spring.

- ❖ For the best and quickest-made leaf-mould, collect beech leaves.

- ❖ Mix grass cuttings with coarser material before putting them in the compost heap, or they will form a sour, wet layer that stops the heap working.

- ❖ Bring seaweed back from seaside expeditions to add to your compost heap. It breaks down to produce potassium and many useful trace elements which will benefit your plants.

- ❖ Make your own wormery from an old plastic dustbin. Bore some drainage holes a couple of inches up from the base, then put 3" (8cm) of gravel in the bottom of the bin and cover it with an old carpet tile to keep the worms out of the gravel. Add a good layer of shredded newspaper with a touch of lime to keep it sweet, then add about 100 brandling worms. You can get them from fishing supply shops. Give them a few days to settle before you start adding layers of fine kitchen waste. When the bin is half full, stop adding material and leave it until all the material has been composted, make a hole in the middle and add damp newspaper for the worms to move into, remove them and empty out the compost before starting again.

- ❖ Avoid putting meat or bones in your compost heap, as this tends to attract rats.

- ❖ Avoid putting cat or dog droppings in your compost heap, as there is a risk of toxocariasis.

- ❖ If you can get hold of fresh manure from horses, farm animals, chickens or pigeons, mix this into your compost heap to encourage it to heat up.

Container growing

- ❖ Brighten up a corner by putting a small clipped box bush in a wide clay pan and surround it with enough thyme plants to form a mat.

- ❖ Dress up the corner of your house by placing a planted trough on each face of the wall so they touch at the corner and appear to wrap round it.

- ❖ To create an attractive area on plain concrete, surround terra cotta pots of plants with big pebbles. The pebbles will help to retain moisture to make a humid atmosphere for the plants.

- ❖ Dress up your drainpipes with clip-on pot holders and pots of your favourite trailing plants.

- Brighten up a dull corner by painting your flowerpots. Use an undercoat of primer before emulsion in the colour of your choice. Experiment with stripes or zigzags, using masking tape to get the edges straight; or use a stencil for patterns.

- Instead of going to the trouble and expense of rooting out old tree stumps, hollow out the centres, drill some drain holes, and use them as planters.

- Take standard marguerite plants into a cool greenhouse for the winter to protect them from the frost. Keep the compost barely moist and repot them in the spring before putting them outside again.

- Make sure you buy frost-proof terra cotta pots. If they don't have a label which says they are frost-proof, and they come from southern Europe, they will be vulnerable to shattering in freezing weather.

- Try an all-white window-box with begonias, pelargoniums, marguerites and white lobelia.

- Break up polyurethane packing into small lumps and use as drainage material in pots instead of crocks or stones.

- For a winter display, plant up tubs or window-boxes with variegated ivy, dwarf conifers, heather, spotted laurel, and bulbs such as aconite or snowdrop, or winter-flowering pansies.

Container growing

- ❖ For spring displays, plant containers in the autumn with bulbs and early-flowering biennials such as wallflowers.

- ❖ Plant perennials directly into the compost, leaving space to insert annual plants still in their pots. Clay pots are best as they will let the plants draw moisture from the surrounding compost as well as what is in their pot.

- ❖ Incorporate slow-release fertilisers in your container compost and forget the worry of regular feeding.

- ❖ Water copiously every day in the spring and summer, even if it has rained. In hot weather be prepared to water twice a day, especially hanging baskets.

- ❖ Arrange containers on your patio with as much care as you arrange the planting in the rest of your garden or they will look stilted and unsatisfactory.

- ❖ Choose small containers rather than large ones which will be too heavy to move easily once they are full of damp compost.

- ❖ Deadhead flowers every day to keep the display going all season.

- ❖ Anchor window-boxes to the window-frame with wire or chain, or fit front brackets to prevent them falling.

- ❖ Make your own window-boxes from ordinary planed deal, held together with brass screws.

Paint it or treat it with timber preservative but not creosote which is poisonous to plants.

❖ For a continuous display in containers, fill the container with gravel and plunge potted plants into it. This makes it easier to replace tired plants without disrupting the whole container.

❖ Half-barrels make attractive tubs, but make sure that the metal hoops are held in place securely or the whole tub could fall apart.

❖ **Hang up a pair of old leather shoes or boots against a wall to use as unusual planters.**

❖ When your old wheelbarrow has become too battered to use, paint the outside and use it as an attractive container or a display stand for potted plants.

❖ Add height to a group of plants in pots by inverting an empty pot and standing a filled pot on top. Alternatively, use piles of bricks to stand the pots at different heights. Either arrangement looks good on a patio or the edge of the drive.

❖ Try growing hostas in hanging baskets or wall-mounted troughs. This solves the slug problem, and looks very effective, especially if the colour of the hosta complements the colour of the wall, for instance a blue-leaved hosta against yellow brick.

❖ For a trouble-free patio display, try a group of dwarf

and prostrate conifers, with tall shapes in tall pots and prostrate shapes in low, wide pots.

❖ Use containers for all those intrusive rooted plants such as variegated ground elder (*Aegopodium podogaria* 'Variegata') that you would love to grow but don't trust not to take over the whole garden.

Cut flowers

❖ Cut flowers in the early morning or late evening when it is cool and their stems are better able to take up water.

❖ Remove any leaves that would otherwise be under water in the vase. This helps to keep the water fresh.

❖ Empty and refill vases with clean water as soon as it shows any sign of discolouring.

❖ Crush the bottom of woody stems to make it easier for them to take up water.

❖ Revive wilting flowers by plunging them up to their heads in warm water until they have recovered.

❖ Some flowers will take up water more easily if you stand them in 1" (2cm) of boiling water for one minute. This method is recommended for roses, hollyhocks, and any plants which 'bleed' when you cut them, such as poppies.

- ❖ **Fill your vases with fizzy lemonade instead of water.** Flowers love it and will last longer.

- ❖ Fill the hollow stems of flowers like delphiniums with water and plug them with wet cotton wool to prevent air locks.

- ❖ Cut peony stems again under running water immediately before putting them in the vase. This prevents air locks and slows the process which leaches the colour out of the flowers.

- ❖ Recut the stems of tulips and hellebores under water and prick the stems at 1" (2cm) intervals with a pin. This will stop them collapsing in the vase.

- ❖ Cut carnation stems between the nodes, as they drink better that way.

- ❖ **To retain the colour in cut snapdragons, put a teaspoonful of sugar in their water.**

- ❖ Leave decorative gourds on the vines until the first frosts, then put them in a cool, airy place to dry for a couple of weeks before varnishing them. Leave a short stem on, as breaking off the stem leaves a wound that is susceptible to rot.

- ❖ Avoid strongly scented flowers if you have asthma sufferers in the family. Pungent scents, such as lily of the valley, can bring on an asthma attack.

- ❖ When you receive gifts of cut flowers, always check them to see if there are any suitable bits

Cut flowers

to take as cuttings. Carnations in particular often have node shoots which are suitable.

❖ Make foxglove 'tea' to add to your cut flower water. Pour boiling water on a handful of leaves and let it steep for several hours before straining it. Throw away any 'tea' that is left over in case anyone tries drinking it—foxgloves contain the poison digitalis.

❖ Add sugar to the water for cut delphiniums and larkspur.

❖ Add charcoal or camphor to the water for daffodils and narcissi.

❖ Keep daffodils in a vase on their own, as they have an adverse effect on other flowers.

❖ Pick nasturtiums and California poppies (*Escholtzia californica*) to enjoy their glowing colours indoors. They only last a few days, but need no special treatment.

❖ Cut clematis for arranging just as the petals are opening. Cut them with 2' (60cm) of stem and stand them in deep water for several hours before recutting them to the desired length as you arrange them. They will last twice as long in plain water as in oasis.

❖ Use only unscented flowers for dining-table arrangements. Over strong scents conflict with the smell of the food and can put people off eating.

- ❖ Avoid using oasis for primroses and polyanthus. They prefer plain water.

Cuttings

- ❖ To make cuttings root without soil, spread a layer of moist sphagnum moss on the top half of a strip of plastic, dip the cuttings in hormone rooting powder in the normal way, add another layer of damp moss, fold up the bottom half of plastic and then roll it up. Fasten it with a rubber band and leave it to root.

- ❖ To encourage carnation cuttings to root, make a small slit in the bottom of the cutting's stem and insert a grain of corn or rice before dipping in rooting powder and potting them. This ensures the cutting holds plenty of rooting powder and speeds the rooting process.

- ❖ Start seed or cuttings of plants for walls or rock gardens in 'Jiffy' pots. These are a small flexible net pots full of compost, and the whole thing can be compressed to push it between cracks.

- ❖ Buy a fresh supply of hormone rooting powder each year as it deteriorates once it is exposed to the air.

- ❖ Use flower arrangers' oasis block to root cuttings. Cut the block into small cubes, make a hole with a skewer or knitting needle, dip the cuttings in rooting powder and insert them into the block.

Once roots are visible, pot them, oasis and all.

❖ Root cuttings of fuchsias and marguerites by standing them in an old glass flower arranging 'rose' in a solution of water and phostrogen.

❖ Take cuttings of daphnes when the flowers have finished, let them dry out for 24 hours and then pot them up in the usual way. Alternatively, cut them as the flowers open and keep them in a vase indoors to enjoy the scent before proceeding as above.

Dahlias

❖ Prepare your dahlia-growing site in the winter with plenty of compost or well-rotted manure. Dahlias are hungry plants and they won't flower well if you starve them.

❖ Always break up last year's tubers before replanting, to avoid overcrowding and spindly blooms. Either plant single pieces of tuber with one shoot, or take cuttings from the shoots.

❖ Before you plant them out, keep an eye on them and move cuttings to bigger pots every time you suspect they are becoming root-bound.

❖ Wait until there is no danger of a late frost before planting dahlias outside.

❖ Support dahlias as soon as they are high enough to do so, as the plant can be snapped off by high winds. Tie each stem to a separate cane to avoid crowding the blooms.

❖ Stop the central stem when it has five pairs of leaves. This encourages side-shoots to develop and give you more flowers.

❖ Grow bedding dahlias from seed, then treat the tubers of your favourites as above to save them for next year.

❖ Stand dahlia tubers upside down for a few days after lifting, to let the stems drain and reduce the risk of rotting in storage.

❖ Stop earwigs damaging your dahlias by putting pots filled with straw at the top of the support canes. Make sure the pots are the highest thing, as earwigs like to climb. Check the pots every day and shake any earwigs out into a bucket of salty water—or better still, transport them to the vegetable garden where they will help control insect pests.

Design

❖ Remember that it's what you like that matters—you're going to have to live with it.

❖ Concrete is a fast and cheap surface for paths and patios. Make it more attractive by running a patterned roller over the surface before it sets, or adding a colour to the mix. You can always add paving later when you can afford it.

Design

- ❖ In a new garden, make sure you know what's there already before starting to dig and plant. Ideally, wait through a whole growing season to see what comes up.

- ❖ Check your aspect—find out how much sun each part of your garden gets at different times of day, and note any areas that are always in the shade. These factors are important when choosing plants or deciding where to put permanent features such as ponds or patios.

- ❖ Work out where the prevailing wind comes from and consider making wind-breaks to shelter tender plants.

- ❖ Wait awhile before you cut down big trees. They may be screening an ugly view, or serving as a wind-break. And they may have a preservation order on them—check with your local council.

- ❖ For a leisure garden for relaxing and entertaining, go for a big patio near the house, and sheltered private areas further away.

- ❖ Consider the architecture of your house when designing your garden. Older or 'period-style' houses look best with soft planting, gentle curves, and textured materials; modern architecture looks better with bold shapes and contemporary materials.

- ❖ Design your garden on paper before you start major structural work such as laying paths or building walls.

- ❖ Make long, narrow gardens look wider by making the path cross at an angle, or taper a central lawn so that it is wider at the far end.

- ❖ Make short, wide gardens look longer by putting the path in the middle, so it draws the eyes away from the sides, or taper a central lawn so it is narrower at the far end.

- ❖ Break up large gardens with hedges, island beds, or groups of trees or shrubs so that the whole garden isn't visible at once.

- ❖ Buy perennial plants and trees in containers and place them in position in the containers until you are sure they are in the right place.

- ❖ Use cheap wire fencing on the boundaries until you can afford something better. Disguise it with annual climbers.

Digging

- ❖ Keep large sheets of heavy-duty polythene to spread on patches you intend to dig. Then rain won't make the ground too wet to get onto.

- ❖ Don't dig so deep that you bring up subsoil. This will be lighter in colour than topsoil and is usually infertile, so it will impede plant growth.

- ❖ Got badly compacted soil, too hard to dig? Hire a pneumatic drill to break it up, put a sprinkler on it for a few hours and then dig.

- ❖ If arthritis or another disability makes digging difficult, buy one of the 'auto-spades' which work from only light pressure on the handle. The spring action lifts and turns the soil for you.

- ❖ Spades without a tread can be uncomfortable to use, so split a piece of old hose and slide it over the edge of the spade.

- ❖ If using a rotavator, vary the depth of penetration by a little every time you dig. This avoids the creation of a hard 'pan' which causes water logging and prevents plant roots penetrating.

- ❖ Reduce your deep digging activities to the strictly essential, which is only when you need to remove deep-rooted weeds or root crops. All other plants survive just as well on shallowly dug soil.

- ❖ **_Spread compost or rotted manure on the surface in late autumn instead of digging it in. The worms will take it into the soil over winter and save you the trouble._**

- ❖ If you find digging difficult, try a longer handle on your spades and forks for better leverage.

Dry flowers

- ❖ Dry flowers for winter arrangements in your microwave oven. Spread them out on kitchen paper, and 'cook' them on the lowest setting for about four minutes, depending on how large they are.

- ❖ To make a simple drying rack to hang bunches of flowers, tie bamboo canes to form a wide 'ladder' and hang or prop this in an airy place.

- ❖ Hang these flowers in bunches to dry: achillea, clarkia, helichrysum, hydrangea, Michaelmas daisies, nigella, poppies, ranunculus.

- ❖ Dry grasses and these flowers in silver sand: dahlias, hellebores, peonies, tulips, zinnias.

- ❖ Dry these flowers in alum or borax: calendula, clematis, forget-me-not, primula, rosebuds, scilla.

- ❖ Dry these flowers in silica gel: gypsophila, periwinkles, primroses, snowdrops, violets, wood-anemones.

- ❖ To decide when flowers and other material are dry enough to use, give them a gentle shake. If they rustle, they're ready.

- ❖ Delicate flowers tend to have stalks which are too weak to hold them up once dry, so cut a piece of corn stem and slip it over the stalk, or wire the flower-head to a fine twig.

- ❖ **To prevent plumed grasses and flowers such as globe artichokes releasing their seed and filling your house with fluff 'fairies,' give them a good spraying with hair laquer.**

- ❖ Dress up a simple bunch of hanging flowers with a bow of pretty ribbon.

Dry flowers

- ❖ Fill a tall glass jar with a mixture of dried flowerheads, pine cones, wisps of unusual grasses and decorative seedpods.

- ❖ Store dried flowers and grasses in dust-proof boxes in a dry place until you are ready to arrange them.

- ❖ Fold up a tissue and poke it in dried flower arrangements, then put a couple of drops of appropriately scented oil on it.

- ❖ To preserve beech leaves, castor oil plant (*Fatsia japonica*), ferns, ivies and rhododendrons for winter decorations, cut slim branches any time after July, split the ends of the stems and remove the lower leaves. Stand them 2" (5cm) deep in a mixture of one-third glycerine and two-thirds water until the leaves take on an oily look, then remove them and make your arrangements.

- ❖ Let herbs such as hyssop, marjoram and thyme flower before cutting them to dry and add pink to arrangements of dried herbs.

- ❖ Look round your vegetable patch for drying material. Leek seed heads and globe artichokes flowers are spectacular in large arrangements, but many other vegetable seed heads have potential.

Edible flowers

- ❖ Check identification before **eating flowers** and don't eat any that you are not sure about.

- Use rose petals or violets for crystalising as cake decorations.

- Spice up your salads with nasturtium flowers (*Tropaeolum majus*). Pick them before the flower is fully open and you'll be able to taste the nectar in the spur behind the petals.

- Make rose flavoured ice-cream by whizzing petals in a food processor and stirring them into plain ice-cream.

- Pull the star-like blue flowers off borage (*Borago officinalis*) to add to summer drinks, or freeze them into ice-cubes.

- Use chive flowers to add a delicate onion flavour to green salads.

- Add elder flowers (*Sambucus nigra*) to gooseberries to perk up a pie, or make a syrup from them for instant elder flower fizz drink. Melt 1 lb (500g) of sugar in 1 gallon (4 litres) of boiling water, add the juice of one lemon and ten flower-heads, let them steep overnight, strain and bottle. Put 1" (2cm) of syrup in the bottom of a glass and top it up with fizzy water. This syrup is also good on ice-cream.

- Sprinkle the flowers of edible herbs over salads or omelettes.

- Chop nasturtium flowers and mix them in with cream cheese for a pretty spread.

- Add unopened buds of day lilies (*Hemerocallis*) to salads for a smokey taste, steam them or add them to a stir-fry.

- Dry the petals of pot marigolds (*Calendula officinalis*) and use them as a substitute for saffron in rice dishes. They don't have as strong a flavour, but they do colour the food.

- You can also eat the flowers of hollyhocks, daisies, pansies, clove pinks (*Dianthus caryophyllus*), fuchsia (*F. magellanica*) and gladioli (*Gladiolus tristus*). Add any of these to a salad.

Eggshells

- Save all your eggshells and crush them finely as a good source of calcium for plants. Mix them with your usual potting compost.

- Use eggshells as seed pots. Just put a little compost and a seed in each shell, then when the plant is ready to be moved on, gently crush the shell and plant the whole thing. This is a good way to give brassicas the lime they love.

- ***Dry off your eggshells in the oven, crush them coarsely, and sprinkle a ring round your tender plants to keep slugs and snails at bay. They hate to crawl over sharp things!***

- Use the empty shells from boiled eggs to grow mustard and cress. Just stand them in an eggcup, add a little compost and the seeds. *If you like, draw a face on them with a marker pen and wait for the 'hair' to grow!*

Evening gardens

❖ Extend your enjoyment of your garden by adding lights to your patio so you can sit out after dark in warm weather.

❖ Choose plants with pale or white flowers that can be enjoyed at twilight.

❖ Go further and choose the pale flowers that give off their scent at night, such as summer jasmine (*J. officinale*), nicotiana, night scented stock (*Matthiolis bicorna*), and angels' trumpets (*Brugmansia comigera)* and evening primrose (*Oenothera biennis*).

❖ Choose other flowers and shrubs that are strongly scented. If you can't see them that well after dark, at least you will be able to enjoy the scent.

❖ Include time-switches in the circuits for your garden lights, so they will come on when you are on holiday, and make burglars think you are still there.

❖ Make sure steps, pools, and other potentially dangerous places are well lit to avoid accidents.

❖ Train spotlights on favourite plants so you can still see them from indoors on chilly or wet evenings. Be considerate of your neighbours when locating spotlights. It is often the upward pointing beams which annoy, when you can often get the same effect from a light which is mounted high up and shining down.

❖ Add extra light for party evenings with wax or oil-filled flares. Make sure children keep a safe distance from these flames.

❖ If you like wild flowers, be sure to include our native bladder campion (*Silene vulgaris*) and white campion (*S. pratensis*). Both give off delicious scent at night.

Fences

❖ Always use plastic coated chain-link fencing, as the uncoated sort can cause a build-up of zinc toxicity in the soil from rain drips. Black plastic coating is less visibly intrusive than green coating.

❖ Avoid creosote as a fence preservative where any plants may touch the fence. Creosote gives off fumes which poison plants.

❖ Buy wooden fencing material that has been pressure-treated with preservatives rather than the less penetrating painting.

❖ When wooden fence posts rot at the base, put a new post in next to them and bolt it to the old post.

- ❖ Use metal post spikes instead of concrete to fix posts into the ground. They are easier and quicker than concrete, and you can add the fence panels immediately instead of having to wait for the concrete to dry.

- ❖ When fences start to lean, wedge a wooden strut against them and plant tall things to disguise the strut.

- ❖ Fit gravel boards to the bottom of fences next to flower or vegetable beds to protect the fence from damp earth.

- ❖ Dress up a plain fence by adding finials to the posts. You can buy these in several designs, or utilise 'found objects' such as large pine cones.

Fertilisers

- ❖ **Mix a batch of liquid fertiliser and freeze it in an old ice-cube tray or plastic ice-cube bags.** Then put a couple of cubes in your pots or tubs when they need feeding. While the cubes are in the freezer, make sure they are clearly labeled and warn the family that they are there.

- ❖ Rather than scattering fertiliser all round plants, draw out a deep drill next to the plants, put the fertiliser in that and cover it again.

- ❖ To make your own organic general purpose fertiliser, mix 3 parts by weight of hoof and horn,

3 parts bone meal, 8 parts of seaweed meal, and spread at 4-6 oz (100g) per square yard.

❖ Use tomato fertiliser for roses and vice versa. The ingredients are much the same, and it saves you having to buy two lots.

❖ Check the composition of fertilisers, and whether they are appropriate to your purpose. For instance, you shouldn't give nitrogen to beans or you'll get luxurious leaves and no beans.

❖ Make your own liquid feed by hanging a sack of nettles or comfrey in a water-butt. Resist the temptation to stir it—it smells dreadful!

❖ Feed tomatoes with Epsom salts to prevent and cure yellow leaves.

❖ **For jumbo plants, try Zoo Poo—manure sold by zoos.**

❖ **Add half can of non-diet cola to a gallon of water as a perk-up feed for your plants.**

Foliage

These are the easiest to grow and most popular foliage plants. Try them yourself: Grey or silver leaves—alchemilla, artemisia, centaurea, cupressus, eucalyptus, euphorbia, salvia, santolina, saxifrage, sedum, sempervivum. Red, purple or copper—bugle, cotinus, bishop's hat, sedum, sempervivum. Yellow or gold—cypress, elder, heather, juniper, privet, robinia, thuja, thyme. Variegated leaves—actinidia, aucuba, bugle, cornus, dead nettle, eleagnus, euonymus, hebe, hosta, ilex, iris, ivy, mint, miscanthus, periwinkle, pittosporum, privet, sage, scrophularia, sedum, thyme.

- ❖ Use the different colours, shapes, and textures of foliage to create year-round interest in your garden.
- ❖ Be sparing with variegated-leaved plants. A couple are attractive, more just look confusing and 'busy.'
- ❖ Use the New Zealand flax (*Phormium tenax*) to create a bold statement of spear-like leaves in a choice of colours.
- ❖ For a contrast of textures, try the deeply cut silvery leaves of cardoon (*Cynara cardunculus*) behind the feathery mid-green summer foliage of asparagus (*A. officinalis*).
- ❖ Choose your favourite leaf colours and use coleus as a bedding plant.
- ❖ Combine bamboos with rodgersias in tones of colour—yellow in both, or green bamboo with purply-red rodgersia.
- ❖ For double value, choose plants with interesting foliage and scent, such as herbs or the sweetbriar rose (*Rosa rubuginosa*).
- ❖ Use large-leaved plants as a backdrop for your favourite flowers.

Frost

❖ Protect tender plants from killing frosts with a covering of straw or bracken held down with a piece of wire netting.

❖ Use fleece over delicate plants such as herbs when severe frost is forecast.

❖ Reduce the harmful effects of frost by spraying water on frosted plants before the sun reaches them.

❖ If your garden is at the bottom of a hill, remember that cold air flows down hill and will collect at the bottom. This may cause a frost pocket against a solid wall. To avoid this, fit an open-work gate in the wall to let the cold air flow through.

Fruit

❖ To grow a peach tree from a stone, bury the stone outside for the winter to give it the cold period it needs, before bringing it in and potting it in the spring.

❖ Save space by growing fruit trees as cordons against a wall or fence, or as a garden divider on wires.

❖ Grow gooseberries as standards, so you can pick the fruit without damaging your hands on the thorns.

- ❖ When buying free-standing fruit trees, check that the varieties you want are available on a rootstock that will produce a tree of the size you want. M27 or M9 are the best for compact trees for smaller gardens.

- ❖ When buying fruit trees, check the pollination situation. Some varieties are self-fertile and do not need another tree to set fruit, but others need another tree of a different variety for cross-pollination.

- ❖ If you are restricted for space, but want to grow two or more varieties of fruit trees, buy a 'family' tree, which has different varieties grafted onto a single rootstock.

- ❖ Remove embryo figs that are any larger than a small pea from the tree in late October. This means the tree can concentrate on maturing the little ones in the following season, instead of putting energy into the bigger ones which will probably have been damaged by cold weather.

- ❖ Choose ballerina apple trees to grow on your patio. They stay compact and need little pruning to retain their upright columnar shape.

- ❖ Support heavily loaded fruit tree branches with an old clothes line prop. This reduces the risk of the weight of fruit tearing the branch off the tree.

- ❖ Crop and prune your blackcurrant bushes in one operation. Blackcurrants produce fruit on last year's new growth, so cut out the fruiting branches and take them to a table where you can pick the fruit off without having to bend and crouch.

❖ Grow a grape vine as a standard in a pot. Simply remove all the side-shoots until the stem has achieved the desired height, then let the top bush out by nipping out the tip. When the embryo bunches have formed, prune the shoots back to two leaves beyond each bunch, leaving only one bunch on each branch, then give a monthly liquid feed until picking time.

❖ Discourage mildew on your grapes by mulching to keep the ground moist, and by thinning the vine to let air circulate. If you do see any signs of mildew, spray with a systemic fungicide.

❖ To tell whether dessert gooseberries are ripe enough to pick, check the colour of the seeds. They turn from yellow to brown when ripe.

❖ Don't bother to 'top and tail' gooseberries and currants before you freeze them. Freeze them loose, bag them up and give them a good shake, when the stems will break off.

❖ **Puzzle your friends with a bottle of pear liqueur containing a whole pear. Just select a suitable pear fruitlet, tie the bottle over it, and wait for the pear to grow and ripen before cutting it and filling the bottle with alcohol and sugar.**

- Use a black plastic bin liner to blanch your rhubarb. Just place the liner over the crown of the plant, weight it down with stones or earth, and wait until you can feel a good length of rhubarb inside before cutting.

- Use 'step-over' cordon apples or pears as low fences for your kitchen or herb gardens.

- Train blackberries, loganberries and other long-brambled fruits over arches for both ease of picking and an attractive feature.

- Grow boysenberries instead of ordinary blackberries. Their flavour is superb, they are prolific fruiters, and they have no thorns.

- Try some of the rarer bramble fruits, such as the tall salmonberry (*Rubus spectabilis*) with magenta flowers and yellow fruits, the tall Japanese wineberry (*R. phoeniculasius*) with amber berries and glowing red fuzz on the stems, or the ground covering strawberry-raspberry (*R. illecebrosus*) or Arctic raspberry (*R. arcticus x stellarticus*).

- For the easiest of fruit trees, choose a damson, ideally one of the self-fertile varieties such as 'Merryweather' or 'Farleigh.'

- Solve the problem of maggots in apples without spraying, by using grease-bands on the main trunk and pheromone traps hung from branches.

- If you are thinking of buying a mulberry tree for fruit, make sure you get a black mulberry (*Morus nigra*) as the fruit of the white mulberry (*M. alba*) is insipid. Alternatives are the rarer more expensive shrub version, the Korean mulberry (*M. autralis*) or hybrids of the American red mulberry (*M. rubra*) and our white mulberry.

- Prune mulberries only in the winter: they can 'bleed to death' from being cut in the growing season.

- To grow your own Kiwi fruits (*Actinidia deliciosa syn. chinensis*) make sure you have both male and female plants. This plant is tender, so only to be attempted in warm and sheltered gardens. The more decorative *A. kolomikta*, known for its pink and white splashed leaves, also has edible fruits, but again you need male and female plants.

- If you heat your greenhouse in the winter or have a conservatory, try citrus fruit. 'Meyers Lemon' is the easiest to grow, but the calamondin orange (*Citrus mitis*) or mandarin orange (*C. reticulata*) are also suitable.

- Grow some autumn raspberries as well as the summer-fruiting ones. Prune the canes to within 6" (15cm) of the ground in April and they will fruit in late August.

- Raspberries grow well in containers, so pot up a few and keep them in the greenhouse to get an early crop.

Fuchsias

❖ Grow your own standard fuchsias by attaching the main stem to a training stake and pinching out all the side-shoots lower than 3" (8cm) from the growing tip. Leave the leaves on as they help strengthen the stem. When it is as tall as you want, pinch out the tip and then the tip of each side-shoot to create a head. Keep it in a warm greenhouse over the winter and in the second year rub off the leaves from the main stem and allow it to flower.

❖ For a strong stemmed standard, choose the cuttings that have leaves in groups of three rather than pairs.

❖ Train a spectacular pillar or pyramid fuchsia by pinching out the tip at 18" (45cm), then selecting one of the resulting two shoots to be the new main stem and pinching that out at a further 18" (45cm). Repeat this twice more. Let each level of side-shoots go far enough to form a pyramid shape. Over the course of several years you should be able to get your column to over 6' (2m) high.

❖ To grow your own plants from cuttings, select young shoots and remove all but the top pair of leaves before putting the cuttings into compost and providing them with bottom heat. They should grow roots in about four weeks, then you can pot them on and start pinching them out as soon as they are established.

- Repot overwintered plants in late February to provoke them into rapid growth, and mist them to encourage the sap to rise.

- Feed fuchsias in hanging baskets regularly with a high potash fertiliser to keep the flowers coming.

- Give your fuchsias plenty of water in the growing season, but don't leave pots standing in a saucer of water.

- Prune hardy fuchsias back to a few inches above the ground as soon as the first shoots appear in spring.

- As winter approaches, push a covering of straw or bracken into the centre of outdoor hardy fuchsias to give them protection against hard frosts.

- Bury your tender fuchsias, pot and all, for the winter. Trim the straggly and dead growth, dig a deep hole and put the whole thing in, cover it and mark it so you can find it again in the spring.

Furniture

- Make a herb seat with chamomile, creeping thymes and creeping mints. Simply build a high sided bed and plant the herbs, then press the growing plants down every week or so to encourage the stems to root down and form a dense mat.

- Site your barbecue close enough to the house to be able to pop in to fetch things without a long trek.

- Choose garden furniture which is robust such as timber benches which can stay outside all year, or go for lightweight furniture which can easily be put under cover when it rains.

- Choose fabrics with care. Bright colours may clash with your plants and flowers and soon become tiresome.

- Put a seat close to the kitchen door, so the cook can sit outside in nice weather and do jobs like shelling peas or peeling potatoes.

- Leave plenty of room round tables for people to get out of chairs without colliding with plants.

- Treat teak and iroko wood furniture with an annual coat of teak oil to prevent rotting.

- Site your garden furniture so that each seat gives the sitter an interesting view.

- Hang a hammock in a shady place for afternoon snoozes or comfortable reading.

Gates

- Ensure that your gate is safely fixed and that the gate posts are sound. You could be sued if your gate collapses and hurts someone.

❖ Choose a gate that complements the hedge, wall or fence in which it is set. If the house is visible from the front gate, the gate could reflect the style of the house.

❖ Pave the path round gates, or a muddy depression will eventually form.

❖ Ensure that gates are wide enough for wheelbarrows and other garden machinery.

❖ Discourage children from swinging on gates. It ruins the hinges and may pull them out of the post.

❖ Avoid overelaborate gates in humble surroundings. They don't look impressive, just pretentious.

❖ If you have a new gate, or a valuable old one, attach it to its posts, and the posts to the ground, in such a way that it cannot easily be removed by thieves.

❖ Use gates within your garden to frame a view and invite the observer to move from one part of the garden to another.

❖ Add a touch of the romantic to your garden with a moongate. Historically, these completely circular openings have been in walls, but there is no reason why you should not have a moongate in a tall fence or hedge.

Geraniums and pelargoniums

- Try hardy geraniums in your borders. They come in a range of colours from white through pinks and reds to deep purple, form dense mats of foliage and flower, and are extremely easy to grow and propagate.

- Grow hybrid zonal and ivy-leaved pelargoniums from seed. Give them a temperature of 72°F/22°C for rapid germination, then keep the seedlings at 62°F/17°C until ready to harden them off to go outside.

- Feed your pelargoniums with tomato fertiliser during the flowering season.

- Keep pelargonium plants moist but not waterlogged.

- Take cuttings between late July and mid-September and keep in warmth over winter. Sever the shoots just below a leaf and remove all but the top leaves before dipping in rooting powder and inserting in compost.

- Use ascorbic acid instead of rooting powder. Use ½ oz (1 g) of ascorbic acid powder to 4 oz (85 ml) of water and keep the solution in a dark bottle, stirring well to mix it before use.

- When you are tidying up your pelargoniums in autumn, cut any remaining flowers and bring them indoors to keep in a vase.

- ❖ For something different, try the double Stellar pelargoniums. Their raggedy petals make them stand out from other varieties.

Gifts

- ❖ For a quickly made gift from your garden, make up a tussiemussie of decorative leaved scented herbs or small flowers tied with kitchen string to hang up, and a ribbon for decoration.

- ❖ For a really exclusive gift, arrange for a plant to be named after the recipient. Check with your local horticultural society to see if there are any amateur plant breeders—they are often stuck for names to give their new varieties.

- ❖ Give gardening friends traditional metal watering-cans, dressed up with a coat of paint and a stenciled motif.

- ❖ If you are going to give plants or rooted cuttings from your garden, repot them into new clay pots and add a ribbon to turn a casual hand-over into a more notable event.

- ❖ Give greenhouse enthusiasts some pest control predators as a gift.

Grasses

- ❖ Confine invasive grasses such as gardener's garters in containers sunk into the soil, as otherwise they can take over the whole bed.

- If you like blue in your garden, try the small mound-forming fescue (*Festuca ovina* 'Blueglow'). Its leaves are powder blue in summer and it produces 12" (30cm) feathery flower spikes.

- To mimic the sea-like effect of a field of barley on a breezy day, plant some clumps of *Stipa tenufolia*.

- Site tall grasses where they will be enhanced by the late afternoon or early morning sun. This is especially effective with grasses that have plumed flower-heads.

- Avoid the gardening cliche of a clump of pampas grass in the middle of the lawn by using it as a backdrop at the rear of a border and choosing one of the more delicate varieties such as 'Pumilla' or 'Aureolineata.'

- To mask ugly sheds, or for use as an 'architectural statement,' try the tall clump-forming zebra grass (*Miscanthus sinensis*). Cross banded in yellow, or edged with white if you choose 'Variegatus,' it makes a tall, green fountain.

- If you need to divide ornamental grasses, do it in spring or summer when they are growing. They tend to die if you disturb them in the winter.

- Keep a bucket of water handy **when you set fire to your pampas grass.** Burning tidies the clump and kills insect pests but if the fire becomes deep-seated it will kill the grass as well.

Green ethics

❖ Use coir compost or shredded bark rather than peat-based products.

❖ Make sure species bulbs have been propagated in nurseries, not collected from the wild.

❖ Only buy rocks that have been quarried, not collected from a natural limestone 'pavement.'

Greenhouses and other glass protection

❖ Install an electricity supply in your greenhouse to give you power for watering systems and propagating units.

❖ Remove automatic window openers in the winter, as heavy frosts can damage the liquid reservoirs which operate them.

❖ Locate greenhouses where they will get plenty of sun in winter and where you can get to them without getting muddy feet.

❖ Grow a pot of basil in your greenhouse to repel whitefly. They don't like the smell.

❖ Keep your greenhouse warm in the winter and save on heating bills by lining it with bubble plastic. The bubbles should be against the glass, to form a solid layer of air.

❖ Make quick cloches with two sheets of glass and four clothes pegs. Put two pegs on each piece of glass, lean the sheets of glass together, and put a rubber band on each pair of pegs to hold them together.

❖ Fix up a clear polythene curtain to separate plants which need different growing conditions such as dry and light for tomatoes or shady and moist for cucumbers.

❖ Water your greenhouse in the morning. Evening watering leaves moist conditions overnight which encourage red spider mite.

❖ Grow vegetable crops in growbags or tubs rather than in the border soil, to avoid a build-up of diseases and pests.

❖ Make your own staging with trestle legs and planks or expanded metal.

❖ If you have children in your garden, choose a cheap plastic greenhouse until they are grown-up, or choose rigid plastic glazing rather than glass.

❖ For cheap adjustable greenhouse shades, use roll-up bamboo blinds.

❖ If using biological pest control methods in your greenhouse, check with the suppliers whether you can use pesticides without killing the predators you've purchased.

❖ Treat wooden structural portions of your greenhouse with linseed oil every five years.

Greenhouses and other glass protection

- ❖ Install a water supply in your greenhouse, even if it is no more elaborate than a tap.

- ❖ Keep a tank in your greenhouse to bring water up to air temperature before using it on your plants. Mains water can be cold enough to shock tender plants in hot weather.

- ❖ If you heat your greenhouse by electricity, keep a small paraffin heater as a backup in case of power cuts.

- ❖ Ask yourself if you really need to heat the whole greenhouse, or whether a propagator would be sufficient to keep your favourite plants going through the winter.

- ❖ Make a cheap cold frame the Chinese way, by digging a pit, lining the sides with sheets of polystyrene, then laying a few bamboo canes across the top to support plastic sheeting for a lid. A layer of gravel in the bottom of the pit will absorb heat during the day and give it off slowly at night.

- ❖ Put cloches out on the growing area at least two weeks before adding plants or seed, to let the soil warm up. Cover the ends to keep out drafts.

- ❖ Cold-frames and cloches attract ants, who like to make nests in warm places, so sprinkle ant killer round the edges to keep them out before they damage your plants.

- Use plastic water-bottles as individual mini-greenhouses for tender plants. Cut off the bottom and push the bottle firmly into the soil over the plant. Pop a few slug pellets inside and put the lid on until the weather warms up.

Green manure

- Run over your green manure with a mower before digging it in. This is much easier than trying to chop it with a spade.

- Avoid using mustard as a green manure if you have clubroot in your soil. Mustard is a brassica and will keep the clubroot going.

- If your green manure plants get too mature to dig in, just pull them up and add them to the compost heap.

- Save your own seed for green manure from common plants. Anything which grows quickly from seed will do, for instance pot marigold (*Calendula*), beans, or even weeds such as fat hen, as long as you dig them in before they seed again.

- Buy spinach seed in bulk for a quick rotting green manure.

- Sow green manure as soon as you empty a space, unless you will be using it immediately. Even three weeks is enough time to get a useful amount of growth of mustard or spinach.

Green vegetables

❖ Keep the pigeons off your cabbages and Brussels sprouts by covering them with the net bags from greengrocers.

❖ Cut cabbages off the stalk and leave the stalk in the ground after cutting a cross in the top of the stalk. Four or five small cabbages will form in the cuts in a few weeks.

❖ Cabbages like to grow in firm ground, so prepare their site early to let it consolidate, then trample all over it to make sure it is really firm.

❖ To keep your Brussels sprouts tight and tasty, stake the plants to stop them rocking in the wind, and earth up the bottom of the stems.

❖ Protect your cabbages from clubroot by burying sticks of rhubarb in the cabbage patch.

❖ Make your own cheap whitefly traps. Paint pieces of board with yellow paint, then spread soft soap on them. Spray it with water occasionally to keep it sticky, and it will soon be covered in trapped whitefly. If you prefer something more immediate, paint and soft-soap an old kitchen colander, **kick a cabbage** and swish the colander through the air to catch the whitefly that you have disturbed. Alternatively, if your cabbage patch is at home, get out an extension lead and the vacuum cleaner, suck up a little malathion or derris dust, kick the cabbages and suck up the whitefly.

❖ Let weeds grow round your cabbages, or plant a ground covering green manure like white clover, to reduce attack by cabbage root flies. Research has shown that the flies lay over 60 per cent less eggs on cabbages surrounded by low growth than cabbages surrounded by clear ground.

Ground cover

These are the easiest to grow and most popular ground cover plants. Try them yourself: aubretia, bergenia, bugle, cornus, cotoneaster, dead nettle, hardy geranium, helianthemum, hosta, hypericum, juniper, mahonia, oxalis, pachysandra, periwinkle, phlox, pinks, polygonum, potentilla, pulmonaria, saponaria, saxifrage, sedum, stachys, thyme, tiarella, vaccinium, veronica.

❖ For a sunny site, use low-growing spreading roses such as 'Max Graf' and 'Gamebird,' or prostrate varieties such as 'Snow Carpet' or 'Flower Carpet.'

❖ Remember that ground cover can also mean slug cover, so take steps to prevent their damaging your plants.

❖ To avoid the 'corporation park' look that comes from large-scale plantings of a single plant, use a variety of plants in different colours, textures and heights.

❖ Add some climbing plants such as clematis to scramble through other plants and give added colour.

❖ Try ligularia (*L. przewalskii*) as a ground cover plant. Its large leaves will form a dense canopy to smother weeds and it produces tall spikes of yellow flowers in mid-summer.

❖ Add colour and interest to your ground cover by choosing plants which flower, or have variegated leaves.

❖ Save money on ground cover plants by buying big specimens and splitting them. Give the pieces a good start by adding some compost to the soil when you plant, or by keeping them in pots until they are established.

❖ Mulch heavily between newly planted ground cover subjects, to discourage weeds until the plants are big enough to smother the weeds on their own.

❖ Underplant your ground cover plants with bulbs to provide a change of scene in spring.

❖ Spot treat any perennial weeds which do appear by painting them with a glyphosate-based weed killer such as Tumbleweed or Roundup.

❖ For ground cover in shady areas, try ivies, bergenia, hostas, pulmonarias, or bugle (*Ajuga reptens*).

Hanging baskets

❖ Buy perennial lobelia (*L. erinus* or *L. angulata*) and keep it from year to year. Cut the plants back to short stems in November, divide the root up, looking for strong buds or shoots, and pot it up until the spring.

❖ To provide hanging baskets with a steady supply of water in hot weather, freeze small plastic bottles of water, then up end them in the baskets to water the plants as they melt.

❖ Use the moss raked from your lawn to line baskets, or use prunings from conifers.

❖ For a simple but attractive spring window-box, try pale pink tulips with white grape hyacinths and some fine leaved ivy like *Hedera helix* 'Sagittifolia.'

❖ Use a 'swagbag' instead of hanging baskets. Line a stout hessian sack with a plastic sack, fill it with compost and tie both ends tightly with stout cord or wire. Leave long enough ends on the cord to hang the basket from two hooks. Insert a length of perforated plastic tube to ensure even watering, then make small slits in the bag to insert plants.

❖ When your hanging basket plants have died down in the autumn, empty the plants and compost out and use the basket as a bird feeder for the winter.

❖ For an early hanging basket display, put pansies round the sides and miniature daffodils, crocuses or grape hyacinths in the top.

❖ Buy a second set of hanging baskets and window-boxes to replace summer displays with ivies and other winter hardy plants.

❖ Replacing the windows in your house? Save the scroll-like fasteners and use them to make hanging basket hooks.

❖ Water copiously every day in the spring and summer, even if it has rained. In hot weather be prepared to water twice a day.

❖ **Grow something edible in your hanging baskets,** like strawberries, 'Tumbler' tomatoes, or purple-podded dwarf beans.

❖ Stand hanging baskets in buckets to hold them steady while you fill them with compost and plants.

Health

❖ When digging on windy days, always face the wind. This prevents chilled back muscles and kidneys.

❖ Always wear knee-pads or use a kneeler if you expect to do a lot of kneeling on hard surfaces, and avoid permanent damage to your knees.

❖ To avoid trouble with your knees, limit kneeling to 15 minutes at a time.

❖ Kneel on both knees with your weight evenly distributed.

- ❖ Wear flexible shoes which allow your feet to bend. This reduces the strain on your knees.

- ❖ Buy a kneeler with hand grips to make getting up easier. Most of these kneelers double as a seat which will let you do a lot of low-down jobs without having to kneel.

- ❖ Make cheap knee-pads or kneelers with rolled strips of bubble plastic.

- ❖ Buy old elbow-length suede gloves to save your hands and arms from scratches when pruning or picking roses or gooseberries.

- ❖ Avoid aggravating your hay fever or asthma by choosing plants which gather dust, and those which are wind-pollinated such as grasses, conifers, and plants in the daisy family.

- ❖ Avoid allergic skin reactions by wearing long sleeves and gloves, and disposing of plants such as euphorbias and rue which are known to cause these reactions.

- ❖ Protect your back from serious strains by learning the correct lifting technique—knees bent and back straight, then using your thigh muscles to stand up, rather than keeping your legs straight and bending your back.

- ❖ Save your back by limiting bending. Organise a table or bench where you can prepare cuttings or separate plants, dig by using your leg muscles and keeping your back straight, and use a seat for low-down jobs rather than bending.

❖ If you have to consult your doctor or a hospital about a plant caused allergy or suspected poisoning, take a sample of the plant with you for accurate identification. In the case of swallowed chemicals, or splashes in the eyes, take the container with you for the same reason. Treatment may depend on the specific cause.

❖ Avoid handling hairy caterpillars, as the hairs contain a skin irritant.

❖ Be prepared for stings from bees and wasps by keeping a pair of tweezers handy to remove the sting and a sting-specific pain reliever spray.

❖ Make sure your anti-tetanus jabs are up to date. The tetanus bug lurks in the soil in most of Britain, and gardeners are particularly vulnerable.

❖ If you have children in your garden, teach them not to eat or handle any plant that you have not approved. For absolute safety, remove poisonous plants such as laburnum.

Hedges

These are the easiest to grow and most popular hedging plants. Try them yourself: beech, berberis, box, cypress, eleagnus, escallonia, forsythia, fuchsia, hawthorn, hornbeam, hypericum, ilex, lonicera, privet, pyracantha, rose species, rosemary, santolina, syringa, tamarix, thuja, viburnum, yew.

- Cut a window in tall hedges to give a view of the scene behind. Make a template of the shape you want and fix it on a stick to establish the correct position. Snip round the edges to mark the shape before cutting a hole right through the hedge in the centre of the window and working outwards.

- To keep the attractive brown leaves on a beech or hornbeam hedge over winter, cut the hedge in late July or early August to encourage new leaf production. Earlier cuts allow the new leaves to mature and fall in autumn, leaving bare stems for the winter.

- Plant violets at the bottom of hedges—their natural habitat in the wild. For a pale-coloured hedge, choose the contrasting effect of the purple-leaved violet (*Viola labradorica*).

- Getting rid of an old hedge? Put plenty of manure into the ground before you try to grow anything else, as the soil is likely to be impoverished.

- ***Want to get rid of a low box hedge? Advertise your intention in one of the gardening magazines and someone will buy it from you—and dig it out themselves!***

- Buy young plants no more than 12" (30cm) high.

They'll settle in much more quickly than older plants and soon catch up in height.

❖ For a denser hedge, plant two staggered rows 15" (40cm) apart rather than the usual single row.

❖ As soon as you have planted your hedge, prune it to encourage the individual plants to bush out.

❖ If the clippings are too woody to go in your compost heap, keep them separate until you start a new heap and put them on the bottom.

❖ Old hedges can be encouraged into new growth by hard pruning. It won't work with box or conifers, but most other hedge plants will respond. Do one side one year and the other side the next year.

❖ Remember to feed hedges. Many people think privet is poisonous because few other plants will survive next to it. It isn't poisonous, just greedy and putting its roots out to grab all the nutrients it can get, starving the other plants in the process.

❖ If you have a tall hedge that is getting tatty, plant some climbers to scramble up and disguise the tatty bits. Hops are particularly useful for this as they die back each year and won't stop you trimming the hedge.

❖ Start a new privet hedge with prunings from an old one. Take woody cuttings 12"-18" (30-45cm) long and push them one third of their length deep into the soil at 6" (15cm) intervals, where you want the new hedge. Keep the soil moist, and put a few into a pot in case any of the others don't make it.

❖ Use your hedge as a burglar deterrent by choosing prickly holly or thorny *Rosa rugosa*. The latter also gives you flowers and attractive hips.

Hedge trimming

❖ If using an electric hedge trimmer, always use a circuit-breaker in case you inadvertently cut the lead.

❖ Drape the lead over your shoulder to keep it away from the blades.

❖ Before you start cutting, make sure there are no hidden obstructions in the hedge to catch on the blades.

❖ Always wear goggles. Hedges tend to collect dust which the cutting disturbs, and the trimmers can throw bits of twig and leaf into your face.

❖ Always wear good stout gloves, ideally leather, to protect your hands from twigs, and from the trimmers themselves.

❖ Don't put yourself in a position where you have to stretch to reach the hedge. If you are standing on something to reach a tall hedge, move it frequently.

Hedge trimming

- ❖ Don't try to cut through thick branches with electric trimmers. Leave them and cut them later with secateurs or loppers.

- ❖ At the end of each season, get the blades of your trimmer or shears sharpened. Keep them well-oiled during the season—sharp tools are easier to use and give a cleaner cut.

- ❖ If you hate hedge trimming, use a hedge growth retardant. Dilute according to the instructions and spray onto the hedge after the first spring clip. Don't use a retardant if there are flowers growing under the hedge, or they'll stop growing too!

- ❖ Before cutting your hedge, spread a long piece of 3' (1m) wide plastic or hessian along the base of the hedge to catch the cuttings. When you've finished cutting, roll up the plastic with the cuttings inside and take it to your compost heap or bonfire site. To empty the roll, just hold the loose ends and give it a good shake.

- ❖ When buying hedging shears, try them for weight and balance. Badly balanced, over-heavy shears are tiring to use.

- ❖ Check that there are no birds nesting in your hedge before you start cutting. If you disturb them they will abandon the nest.

- ❖ Think of all the people you hate when you are cutting your hedge and imagine that you are chopping off their heads!

Herbs

- Grow intrusive rooted herbs such as mint in lengths of builders' red sewage pipe. Cut the pipe into different lengths with a stonecutter (from a hire shop) and bury one third of the pipe, arranging them in a pleasing group of different heights. Fill them with compost and plant the herbs in the top.

- Grow culinary herbs where they can be easily reached from the path. Cooks in a hurry want to dash out and grab a sprig of herbs without having to change shoes.

- When sage plants have become leggy, propagate new plants by covering the old plant with a mound of earth, leaving just the tips showing. Each branch will produce roots in a couple of months and can then be severed and planted out.

- Propagate new shrubby herbs such as thyme and rosemary by taking softwood cuttings in autumn.

- When starting a new herb garden, leave plenty of room for the plants to spread. Fill the gaps with annual herbs such as summer savory or basil.

- Confine the roots of mint, or it will run underground and take over the whole garden. Either sink bottomless buckets into the soil, or grow it in a tub above ground.

Herbs

- ❖ Traditional herb gardens have low hedges of box round the beds. For something different, make your hedges of cotton lavender (*Santolina virens*), lavender (*Lavendula officinalis*) or in warm sheltered gardens, rosemary.

- ❖ Grow the shrubby Mediterranean herbs such as lavender, rosemary, thyme or fennel, on a stony bank. This mimics their natural habitat.

- ❖ Grow your herbs in a checkerboard of beds left between paving slabs to keep them apart and give a modern appearance.

- ❖ If all you want in the way of herbs is some mint for your lamb and potatoes, grow it in a growbag.

- ❖ Put a seat in your herb garden so you can enjoy the scent on warm days.

- ❖ Grow creeping herbs such as wild thymes, creeping mints and chamomile in the cracks in your paths. They don't mind being trodden on and will actually spread better because treading on them presses their stems onto the soil where they root down. You can also grow them on top of a low wall to make a herb seat.

- ❖ *If you want to grow the statuesque clary sage (**Salvia sclarea**), put it where you won't brush past it. It has a strong scent of sweaty armpits, which is why it used to be called 'Hot Housemaid'!*

- ❖ For a really attractive herb garden, choose the coloured or variegated versions of common herbs. Mint comes in purple, white-striped or yellow-striped form; sage can be purple-, grey-, yellow-striped or white-, purple- and green-striped; thyme and rosemary both come in variegated forms—and they all have a slightly different taste.

- ❖ Create a knot garden quickly by taking cuttings and inserting them into the ground in your desired pattern. They should root down in place, but put a few extras in pots to fill in any gaps.

- ❖ Spread some extra herb plants round the garden to take advantage of their ornamental characteristics, instead of confining them all to a bed near the kitchen.

- ❖ For the most flavoursome mint tea, grow Moroccan mint (*Mentha spicata* 'Moroccan'). Pot some up in the autumn and keep it in the greenhouse or on the kitchen window-sill for a winter supply.

- ❖ To make an attractive miniature herb garden, lay four decorative concrete screen blocks on the soil, fill the gaps with compost and plant a herb in each hole.

- ❖ Keep a pot of basil or thyme in your kitchen to repel flies.

- ❖ Plant ground-hugging herbs such as wild thyme

and chamomile round your clothes drying area and enjoy their scent underfoot as you hang out the washing.

❖ Blanch your garlic chives for use in winter. Choose a day when the leaves are dry, cover them with a tall pot or piece of drainpipe and cover the end to keep out the light. They should be ready to use in two weeks.

❖ Coriander tends to bolt in hot weather, so grow it in spring and autumn rather than summer. Buy your seed from Suffolk Herbs, who offer different varieties for leaf or seed production. Telephone 01376-572456 and ask for their catalogue.

❖ For cooking, make sure you buy French tarragon (*Artemisia dracunculus*) rather than the easier to grow but virtually tasteless Russian tarragon (*A. dracunculoides*). Buy it as a young plant and crush a leaf to check the strong aniseed-like scent. French tarragon will not grow from seed in this country.

❖ Take potted bay trees inside for the winter as they will not survive frozen roots. Established bay trees grown in the garden soil may be damaged by a severe frost, but will usually shoot again from the base.

❖ Grow broad-leaved parsley rather than the curly-leaved sort. It germinates easily and has a much better flavour.

- ❖ If you're interested in medicinal herbs, visit the Chelsea Physic Garden when you're in London. Check opening times on 0171 352 5646. Grow a selection of herbs in a window-box or hanging basket outside the kitchen door.

- ❖ Don't be tempted to use the herbs you grow for medicinal purposes without consulting a professional herbalist.

- ❖ As a change from ordinary chives, the garlic chive (*Allium tuberosum*) will self-seed quickly to form large clumps. It produces a pompon of star-like white flowers in August and September as well as edible garlic-flavoured strap-like leaves.

- ❖ For bumper crops of lavender, give it plenty of lime.

Houseplants

These are the easiest to grow and most popular. Try them yourself: African violets, aspidistra, begonia, calceolaria, cineraria, clivia, coleus, cyclamen, dieffenbachia, dracaena, ficus, gardenia, hippeastrum, ivy, monstera, philodendron, sanseveria, schlumbergera, tradescantia.

- ❖ Give your Swiss cheese plant (*Monstera deliciosa*) some support or it will sprawl all over the place. A moss pole which can be kept damp is best, as the aerial roots will work their way into this.

- Keep palms out of direct sunlight, and repot them only when they are completely pot-bound.

- When cutting leaves to propagate houseplants, use a very sharp knife, as a blunt knife will cause bruising which can lead to rot.

- If you have a water-softener fitted to your water supply, use bottled water or rainwater for your houseplants.

- Water your air plants well once a day with a mist sprayer, occasionally adding a weak liquid feed to the water.

- Grow your own houseplants with pips from your fruit bowl. Cherimoya, pawpaw, mango, passion fruit, pomegranate and date all make attractive plants as well as the better known avocado.

- Insectivorous plants such as Venus fly trap prefer soft water, so give them boiled tap water, distilled water, or rainwater.

- Plant a selection of low-growing succulents in a bonsai dish, choosing types with contrasting leaf shape and colour.

- Grow hyacinths and narcissus indoors without compost by putting the bulbs in a deep bowl filled with pebbles. Water them as usual. Heel them in outside when they've finished flowering.

- Keep your coconut palm healthy with a daily spraying of tepid water.

- ❖ Don't buy houseplants from pavement displays, especially in the winter. They will be suffering from the effects of cold, wind and exhaust fumes, and may never recover.

- ❖ Choose plants that are suitable for the position they will live in. Consider light, drafts, temperature, and humidity.

- ❖ If you have to move plants, wait until they have finished flowering, or they may drop their buds. Christmas cacti are notorious for this.

- ❖ Water according to the instructions on the label—and no more. Over watering kills more houseplants than any other cause.

- ❖ Feed houseplants in the spring and summer only, unless the label says otherwise. Most need a winter rest without fertiliser.

- ❖ Keep your potted jasmine and stephanotis (*S. floribunda*) in your bedroom, and let their scent ease the stress of your day and soothe you to sleep.

- ❖ Repot your amaryllis lilies (*Hippeastrum*) no more frequently than every four years—they resent having their roots disturbed and won't flower in the year they are repotted.

- ❖ Propagate Cape primrose (*Streptocarpus*) from a fleshy leaf. Cut the leaf into strips, with a piece of the central rib in each bit and gently push the bits into a tray of compost, with the side that was nearest the plant buried. After a couple of months, new plants will have formed on the leaf edges and these can then be potted on.

❖ Encourage poinsettias to colour up again by keeping in complete darkness for 10 hours a day from mid-September to mid-December. When they have finished flowering and dropped all their colourful leaf-bracts, cut the stems back and be sparing with water for a couple of months, then water again as usual.

❖ If you put your houseplants outside in the summer, keep them out of the sun. You may think they will like it, but many will get scorched leaves and die on you.

❖ Stand a chunk of tufa in a shallow bowl of grit and use it to grow mounds of moisture-loving plants indoors. Mind-your-own-business (*Helxine soleirolli*) and mother-of-thousands (*Saxifraga sarmentosa*) are good subjects for this treatment.

❖ To provide a support for tall pot plants, straighten out a wire coat-hanger, bend one end into a spiral or loop, push the straight end through the hole in the pot and sit the pot on the spiral before adding compost and plant.

❖ **Resurrect sick ferns with a dose of castor oil.** Add 1 tablespoonful each of the oil and children's shampoo to 2 pints (1 litre) of warm water, then give each plant 3 tablespoonfuls of the mixture.

- When you put houseplants outside for the summer, put a mothball in each pot to repel pests you don't want to bring into the house when the plants come back in.

- To prevent water-spills from hanging plants staining your carpets, stand another plant underneath.

- Save the water from boiled eggs to give your African violets the calcium boost they like at flowering time.

- **Do talk to your plants.** While you do so, you are giving them a booster dose of the carbon dioxide you exhale.

- To encourage stephanotis (*S. floribunda*) to flower, give it plenty of natural indirect light in a draft-free place, and raise the humidity by misting it regularly. Let the compost dry out completely in between waterings and feed it fortnightly in the growing season.

- Use dry-cleaners' bags to keep your plants moist when you go on holiday. Put a wire coat-hanger in the bag, hang it up over the plants and drape the bag round them after watering. Fix the bottom of the bag so condensation doesn't run out.

- Poinsettias failed to colour up? Colour them quickly with a tin of car spray paint—it won't do them any lasting damage if you prune those leaves off after a couple of weeks.

❖ Make a lily of the valley cone for special occasions. Make a tall cone of chicken-wire, line it with moss and insert the lily corms so that the shoots go through the holes in the wire, filling it with compost as you go. When it is full, fasten a circle of chickenwire over the open end, give it a good soaking and turn it the right way up. Cover it with a large bucket to exclude the light. When the shoots are grown enough to see the flower buds, take off the cover and place it on a saucer for display.

Lawns

❖ For the fastest lawn from seed, try pre-germinated grass seed. Sold as 'liquid sod,' it should be ready for its first trim two weeks from sowing.

❖ To create a scented thyme lawn, choose varieties of *Thymus serpyllum*, the creeping thyme. 'Albus' has white flowers, 'Pink Chintz' or 'Annie Hall' have pink flowers, 'Lanuginosus' pale mauve flowers and 'Coccineus' purple-red flowers. Plant it out at 3" (8cm) spacing between October and March, then in following years divide the plants in August or September to extend the lawn.

❖ If cracks appear in your lawn in dry weather, brush sharp sand into the cracks. This will improve both the appearance and the drainage, since the problem is caused by a high clay content in the soil. For a more permanent solution, spike the lawn in autumn and top-dress it with a mixture of peat and sand.

❖ Use an open space on your lawn to make a sun-clock. Mark a standing place in the centre, then mark where your shadow falls at the different hours with clock golf numerals, flowerpots or selected plants.

❖ Get rid of leather-jackets (crane-fly larva) in lawns by trapping them. Soak the lawn with water, then cover it overnight with thick cardboard or black plastic. In the morning, take up the covering and collect up the leather-jackets that have come up to the surface.

❖ Use the first four mowings after you've used hormone weed killers on your lawn as mulch. Dry them out first and leave them to mature for six months. They shouldn't go on the compost heap.

❖ **Mower bad at starting? Try praising it loudly as you approach it, saying what a splendid mower it is and how easily it starts. This works, much better than swearing or kicking it.**

❖ If you hate cutting the lawn, replace the grass with white clover: It will stay green in dry weather, provide a thick surface for children to play on, and never needs cutting.

❖ If you want a new lawn in a hurry and don't mind the expense, buy turf rather than sowing grass seed.

You can start using a turf lawn in less than a month.

- Keep a newly turfed lawn moist, or the turfs will shrink and leave gaps.

- If starting your lawn from seed, make a seed sprinkler from two plastic flowerpots. Put one inside the other and twist them so the holes aren't quite aligned, but are open enough to let the grass seed through when you shake the pots.

- If you like stripes on your lawn, arrange your cutting so that the last strip ends close to where you store your mower.

- Control moss in your lawn by aerating the soil. This involves driving a fork or other spiked tool into the ground at regular spacing.

- Take the backache out of spiking your lawn with a pair of spiked sandals. Strap them on and stamp up and down—great for working off a bad temper!

- Always remove mowings from the lawn as they encourage worms, which encourages moles. Mowings also impede growth by blocking out light and air and may contain weed seed.

- Feed your lawn in showery weather in spring once the grass is growing strongly. If it doesn't rain for two days after you've applied the fertiliser, put a sprinkler on for a couple of hours to water it in gently.

- ❖ Get rid of the 'thatch' of dead material that builds up in your lawn by 'scarifying' it in September or early spring. For large lawns, hire a power scarifier; otherwise use a rake to scratch the thatch out. Save the moss you rake out of your lawn to line hanging baskets.

- ❖ Apply weed killers several days after mowing and at least four days before the next cut. Lawn weed killers are selective, that is to say, will kill everything except grass, but they need leaf surfaces for absorption into the plant.

- ❖ To kill moss, apply chemical mosskillers or lawn sands in autumn or early spring.

- ❖ Make your own stepping-stones with bricklayers' mortar mix and some 12" (30cm) plastic pot saucers. Spread a little petroleum jelly over the inside of the saucer before mixing the mortar with enough water to make a thick pouring consistency. Pour it into the saucers and stir a little to remove any air bubbles. Let it dry for three or four days before removing the saucer.

- ❖ Kill fairy rings by watering them with a solution of Epsom salts.

- ❖ In dry seasons, adjust your mower to leave longer grass for a lawn that will stay green instead of turning brown.

The magic words

❖ Encourage new plants to grow by telling them "You'll like it there" when you plant them. If they don't obey you, and start looking poorly, it's time for serious stuff. Tell them "Grow, you blighter—or it's the compost heap for you!"

Minimum maintenance gardens

❖ Use hard surfacing materials and plant only 'easy-going' shrubs.

❖ Alternatively, lay the whole area as lawn with a few hedges and trees to give it some shape. Grow a different kind of hedge on each side of the garden for a simple colour effect.

❖ Make your hedges of easy-going shrubs which can be clipped once a year to retain their shape. Choose Mexican orange (*Choisya ternata*), viburnum (*V.tinus*), firethorn (*Pyracantha*), or one of the bush roses which has attractive hips after flowering.

❖ Keep a path cut in the grass and let the rest grow long until late summer. Add wild flowers and bulbs to the long-grass areas.

❖ When buying trees or shrubs for a low maintenance garden, choose those which will give different displays in different seasons. The ideal will have attractive flowers in the spring, good-coloured leaves in the summer, good leaf coloration in autumn, and interesting bark or fruit in the winter. For example, rowan, medlar, crab-apple, hawthorn, maple, dogwood, or spindleberry.

- ❖ If choosing evergreens, include some variegated forms, as too many dark greens can be depressing on damp winter days.

- ❖ For solid hedges, choose hedging plants that only need cutting once a year, such as yew, box, holly or beech. Avoid privet which needs several cuts a year.

- ❖ For some lower splashes of colour, choose herbaceous perennials which need no maintenance other than removal of dead leaves in the winter, such as day lilies, Iris siberica, tall grasses, lupins or peonies.

- ❖ Cover bare ground with mulches and say goodbye to weeding.

- ❖ Grow ground covering plants and shrubs, such as hypericum or prostrate juniper.

- ❖ **Cement the whole area and lay artificial grass with plastic flowers!**

Money from your garden

- ❖ Sell organically grown vegetables, herbs, or fruit to your local restaurants, health food shops, or private caterers.

Money from your garden

- ❖ Sell fresh or dried cut flowers and prunings from your conifers to private commercial flower arrangers.

- ❖ Offer a flower arranging service yourself.

- ❖ Join organisations such as the Women's Institute, or local horticultural societies so you can sell plants at their annual plant sales.

- ❖ Hold your own private plant sale once or twice a year.

- ❖ If you are raising plants for sale, organise a proper watering system for both the growing and display areas. Watering with cans is a waste of time which you could be spending on something more productive.

- ❖ If you have sufficient land, grow something unusual as a 'Pick Your Own' crop, for instance cob nuts or lavender.

- ❖ Make sure plants for sale are correctly labeled with their Latin names.

- ❖ Open your garden to the public. Check with your local council how many days a year you can do this without needing planning permission.

- ❖ Buy your pots and other supplies from wholesalers. Cooksons Plantpak Ltd of Burnham Road, Munden, Maldon, Essex CM9 6NT are extremely helpful.

- Buy a plastic walk-in tunnel for 15' (5m) by 60' (20m) of cold 'greenhouse' to give you a longer growing season and storage space for about a third of the cost of a conventional greenhouse.

- Build up a clientele of private buyers for gourmet vegetables and offer a 'we pick it fresh when you want to cook it' service.

- Prepare hanging baskets for sale in spring, and again in autumn.

- Exhibit dried flower pictures for sale in a local cafe, or your local library.

- Specialise in unusual plants which will bring a premium price, whether sold at plant sales or by mail order.

- Check with your local council before selling edible products such as jam or herb vinegars. You could be fined if you fail to comply with the various regulations on food productions and weights and measures.

- Sell your expertise by lecturing to groups and societies, or by writing articles for newspapers and magazines.

- Offer a gardening service to people who can't, or don't want to, do it themselves. This also gives you an opportunity to sell plants you have raised yourself.

❖ Offer a specialised gardening service, doing tasks that people either dislike such as weeding, or are nervous about doing such as pruning.

❖ Offer a garden planning service to property developers as well as private garden owners. Buy one of the garden design computer packages for ideas and professional looking drawings.

❖ Breed your own varieties of popular flowers such as dahlias, and pass them on to a commercial grower for a licence fee.

❖ Check prices at your local garden centre or plant stalls. If you can't match their wideness of choice, you'll need to beat their prices to attract customers.

❖ Consider the best season to sell any given type of garden product. For instance, bedding and many other young plants for the general gardener will only sell in late spring or early summer.

❖ If you live outside town and have a place where cars can pull off the road, put up a table to sell flowers, pots of plants, etc. Locate the table where you can keep an eye on it from the house and pop out regularly to collect money.

❖ If you want to grow items for sale on an allotment, check that the rules will allow you to.

❖ If you're thinking of growing bedding plants to sell at boot fairs, be warned that the authorities think this constitutes trading and may stop you. You can sell a few plants if you've propagated more than you need, but don't try to do it too often.

❖ Barter your spare garden produce with non-gardening neighbours. You give them beans or sweetpeas, they give you oranges, or a haircut, or fix a fuse, or knit you a sweater.

❖ Make sure there are no restrictive covenants in the deeds of your house or mortgage agreement to prevent your carrying on a trade from home.

❖ If you want to expand your business to make a living from your gardening, see if you can get a business start-up grant.

❖ Keep records of all your expenses to offset against your profits and reduce your tax bill.

Mulching

❖ Use black plastic as a mulch in the kitchen garden for strawberries, potatoes, marrows and other plants which can be planted through a hole cut in the plastic.

❖ Lay mulches after rain when the soil is moist, as subsequent light rain will not reach the roots.

❖ Keep mulching materials a few inches away from tender shoots and stems beloved of slugs, and lay slug-pellets regularly.

- Use organic mulches of shredded bark, spent hops or coco shells round shrubs or in borders where you will not be sowing seeds. The process of decomposition of the mulch ties up nitrogen and hinders germination.

- Avoid peat as a mulch. If it dries out it is extremely difficult to rewet, and rain will run off without benefiting the plants.

- **Use old newspapers as mulching material.** If you can shred them, so much the better.

- Use a thick mulch of straw or bracken to keep the soil diggable round root vegetables in winter. Carrots can be damaged by heavy frost, but parsnips and leeks keep best in the ground.

- If using grass cuttings as mulch, spread them out to dry before putting them round plants, as fresh cuttings tend to heat up and ferment.

Noise

- Block out noise from roads or neighbours with tall, solid hedges or big trees.

- Reduce the irritation of aircraft noise by putting a pergola over your sitting area and training dense climbing plants over it.

- Provide nicer sounds with fountains or plants which rustle in the wind, such as poplar trees or bamboo.

❖ If your neighbours make excessive noise that prevents you enjoying your garden, keep a record of occurrences, with times and durations, before going to your local council for help. However, this can lead to major feuds, so it is best to approach the offenders yourself and politely ask them to reduce the volume.

Nuts

❖ Wear gloves when picking up fallen walnuts. The juice in the husks is a powerful brown dye which will stain your hands for several days.

❖ Prune walnut trees only to remove dead or crossing branches, and then only in April or August, or they will leak sap for many days and can 'bleed to death.'

❖ Perk up an old walnut tree by making holes round the circumference of its drip line and filling them with a handful of granular fertiliser. The holes should be 6" (15cm) deep and 3" (8cm) across.

❖ Keep squirrels off your nut bushes by growing them as standards with the main stem at least 6' (2m) high, and wrap the stem with a piece of slippery plastic to stop the squirrels climbing. To prevent them jumping into the bush from other trees, maintain a gap of at least 8' (2.6m).

❖ If you have space, consider a fruit and nut hedge, with a mixture of almonds and hazels, crab-apples, sloes, damsons or bullace plums, elders and rowans.

❖ For the best crops, make sure you buy named varieties of nut trees.

❖ Choose the sweet chestnut (*Castanea sativa*) variety 'Marron de Lyon' for large nuts produced at an early age.

❖ Rather than the native hazelnut (*Corylus avellana*) choose the filbert (*C. maxima*). This produces larger nuts, and the best varieties are 'Kentish Cob,' 'Lamberts Filbert,' 'Halle Giant' or 'Longue d'Espagne.'

❖ For a dual purpose crop and ornamental filbert, choose the dark red leaved 'Purpurea.'

❖ Try the new trazelnut (*Corylus avellana x colurna*). It's a cross between our native hazel and the Turkish tree hazel. The nuts are like hazels but produced on a full sized tree which has extra long catkins as an attractive feature.

Onions and other edible alliums

❖ Buy onion and shallot sets that have been heat-treated to prevent them putting up a flower spike. Onions that do this will not keep as well.

❖ Get your onion sets in the ground as soon as the weather permits. Onions go through a growth cycle that involves putting on top growth until there are a certain number of hours of daylight, then switch to making a bulb. If you plant them late, they don't have time to get to a decent size.

❖ Buy more onion sets than you need, and plant them closer than the recommended spacing. Then pull alternate onions when they get to be big enough to use as spring onions.

❖ Plant onion sets so they are covered by the soil rather than with their necks sticking out. This prevents them being pulled out by birds, and makes no difference to the size of the crop.

❖ Keep your onion seeds cool. You can grow overwintering onions by sowing the seed in August, but shade the seed-bed in hot weather as they will not germinate at over 70°F/21°C.

❖ For bigger leeks, leave the roots on when transplanting instead of trimming them, and fill in the hole instead of leaving it. The best way to fill in the hole is with a stream of water to wash the soil in.

❖ Give your shallot and onion sets a little twist as you plant them, to set them more firmly in the ground and prevent them being dislodged by their growing roots or interfering birds.

❖ Save your back when dibbing holes for leeks by screwing a shelf bracket to a broom handle and using the bracket as a footrest to push the dibber down.

❖ To get one big clove of garlic instead of several smaller ones, plant the cloves in March. Otherwise, plant the cloves in October.

Open Day—letting the public into your garden

❖ Start by contacting one of the charities that benefit from garden open days for their advice. The biggest is the National Gardens Scheme, whose handbook is available in bookshops and news agents. Alternatively, telephone 01483-211535 and ask for details of your local organiser.

❖ Enlist plenty of family and friends to cope with the visitors. You'll need people to take money, sell plants, sell drinks and cakes, and to stroll round the garden and chat to visitors.

❖ **Keep an eye open for the dreaded 'finger blight'**—people who steal pieces of plants for cuttings. Be especially wary of those who have capacious pockets, large bags or umbrellas.

❖ Make a plan of your garden, with all the plants listed and details of where they can be purchased. Sell these plans at the entrance.

❖ Put plant labels where they can be read from the paths, or people will step on the beds to read them. Choose labels that are too big to be slipped into a pocket—the lazy visitor's method of remembering what plants they fancied.

- ❖ Keep the house locked and all the curtains drawn, to prevent theft either on the day or later. Don't let anyone into the house, not even to go to the toilet.

- ❖ If offering refreshments, avoid cream as it can quickly go 'off' in hot weather.

- ❖ Keep a visitors' book for comments. Some of these will be helpful for future open days. Ignore the catty ones.

- ❖ Propagate plants for sale, on a ratio of three-to-one of easy-to-difficult to grow.

- ❖ Be prepared for visitors to buy enough plants to need a box to carry them.

- ❖ Keep a book for phone numbers of people who would like plants you don't have available on the day.

- ❖ The charity organisers supply sets of tickets, posters, signs and other useful items. If you are going it alone, lay in a stock of these items in advance.

- ❖ Advertise the open day with small posters in your local library, garden centres and florists.

Orchids

- ❖ Choose a cymbidium for your first attempt at orchid growing. These are easy to grow and comparatively easy to get into flower.

- Keep your orchids in an even temperature and a damp atmosphere. Rooms with gas fires are not suitable unless the flowerpot sits on a tray of moist pebbles.

- Keep a supply of rainwater for your orchids.

- Try germinating orchid seed by using the 'mother pot' system. This used to mean sowing seed on the top of a pot already containing a similar orchid, but you can also take some compost from such a pot and put it in a new pot. Put a clean cotton handkerchief on top of the compost, sprinkle the seed on it and put a pane of glass on top. Keep the whole thing moist while you wait for the seed to grow, but don't be too hopeful—orchids are notoriously difficult to grow from seed.

- Use proper orchid fertiliser. In emergencies, use liquid fertiliser in twice the recommended water.

- Once your orchids have flower spikes, keep the plant in the same position. If you turn it, the spike will twist to follow the light.

Ornamental kitchen gardens

- Take another look at edible plants to assess their potential as ornamental plants. For instance, consider the architectural qualities of columnar fruit trees, cardoons and sweet corn, or the textural qualities of carrot foliage and onion leaves.

- ❖ Grow unusual varieties of everyday food plants, especially those with attractive colours, for instance red Brussels sprouts, white-flowered runner beans or golden courgettes.

- ❖ Split your plot into four squares and grow crops in rows set diagonally across each square, using high and low plants to form a bowl or pyramid effect, depending on whether the height is in the outer corners or the centre.

- ❖ While it is possible to grow a few edible items in amongst ornamentals, for serious food production and a better looking kitchen garden, go for a formal pattern of beds laid out in a parterre.

- ❖ Make attractive mini-gardens of 3' (1m) squares of salad vegetables. One square this size would support one tall centre plant and two concentric squares of lower plants.

- ❖ Stick to beds in simple shapes such as squares and rectangles, as other shapes are difficult to hoe and fill with plants. The acute angles of triangles are particularly tricky.

- ❖ Make your parterre pattern of raised beds with attractive corner posts which can serve as net supports.

- ❖ Divide up your plot with cordon fruit trees. 'Stepover' cordons make particularly attractive low boundaries.

❖ With the exception of root vegetables which must be sown in their growing position, start all plants in trays or plug-packs and transplant them. This means you never need have an empty bed, or gaps caused by germination failures.

Paths and steps

❖ Ensure that path and step surfaces do not become slippery when wet. Remove moss and mud regularly.

❖ Use a wide flight of steps as a display stand for your favourite potted plants.

❖ If using bricks for paths and steps, ensure they will be frost proof. The toughest are engineering bricks.

❖ Take the trouble to make good edges to your paths. Victorian rope-edged tiles are expensive, but bricks sunk diagonally into the soil make an attractive edge, as do larch poles or sawn logs.

❖ Use stepping-stones to make an informal path across your lawn.

❖ Ensure that paths which will be used for wheelbarrows are wide enough for the legs as well as the wheel.

❖ Check with your local council to see if they're selling cheap loads of broken paving slabs.

- Sawn-up logs make an attractive informal path but can be slippery when wet. Score them with a criss-cross pattern to provide grip, or nail chicken-wire across the top.

- To avoid dazzle when lighting paths, use lamps which can be directed downwards.

Patios

- Make sure your patio is big enough for what you want to do with it. If you are planning to use it as an outdoor dining area it will need to be bigger than if you just want to put a small seat on it.

- Link your patio's surface to the construction of the house. Echo brick walls with bricks laid as paving, or stone slabs could continue round to connect up with the drive.

- If you're planning a patio close to a pond, keep a good supply of insect repellent handy.

- Choose a patio surfacing material that will not become slippery when wet, and that will not stain irrevocably if someone drops a greasy sausage onto it.

- If your patio is to be connected to the house, make sure it is not higher than the damp-course of the house.

- Add screens of trellis or tall plants to provide privacy.

❖ Provide a slight slope to the surface to allow for good drainage, especially when you will be growing potted plants on your patio.

❖ Fit a small fountain close to your patio to provide the refreshing sound of running water on lazy summer days.

Pests

❖ Keep blackfly off your beans by planting nasturtiums next to the beans. The blackfly prefer the nasturtiums and leave the beans alone.

❖ **To repel vampires as well as aphids,** spray plants with garlic tea. Pour 2 pints (1 litre) of boiling water over four crushed garlic cloves, and let the mixture cool before straining.

❖ Provide a shady place for pests to hide in during hot weather by watering a patch of ground and covering it with a plank or old dustbin lid. Then go back in the evening to dispose of them.

❖ Keep an eye out for the vine weevil. It is dull black, about ½" (1cm) long and has a pronounced snout. If you spot one, check your houseplants for the grubs before they do uncurable damage. Take the plant out of its pot to check the roots. If you find any grubs, wash off all the compost and repot the plant in fresh compost. Pour boiling water over the infested compost before disposing of it.

- Take action as soon as you spot evidence of any pests on your plants. The longer you leave it, the more difficult pest attacks are to control.

- Detect the difference between pests and useful predators by their speed of movement. As a general rule: if it moves fast, it's a friend; if it moves slowly, it's an enemy.

- Reduce the risk of slug damage to seedlings by raising them in trays or plug-packs and planting them out when they are well developed and less tender.

- **Leave some beer in the tins and half bury them to trap slugs.** They climb in for the beer, fall in and drown.

- If you don't want to lay bait for slugs and snails, augment your beer traps by night-time **torchlit slug hunts.**

- Catch slugs in empty orange or grapefruit skins, laid face down on the soil.

- Mix only as much insecticide as you need to use. It loses its effectiveness quite quickly if left to stand.

- Rub a sprig of mint on your wrists to repel mosquitoes.

- Save the flower-heads from sunflowers when the birds have eaten all the seeds and put them face down on the soil. They will fill up with earwigs and woodlice which you can then dispose of.

- Hang a piece of ham fat for the blue tits amongst your rose bushes. They'll pick the aphids off the roses while they queue up for their turn at the fat.

- To discourage ants, plant tansy or lavender.

- Use pressure sprayers when spraying against plant pests. Many of them lurk underneath the leaves which are difficult to reach with non-pressurised sprayers.

- **For the most effective bait in mousetraps, use pumpkin or marrow seeds.**

- Make your own trap for codling moths with waxed paper milk cartons. Mix equal quantities of treacle, vinegar and water and put 1" (2cm) in each carton before hanging them in your apple trees.

- Scare bird pests off your fruit and vegetables by hanging up items which glitter or make a noise. Aluminium pie plates, strips of foil or plastic are all useful for this purpose.

- Catch raspberry beetles before they lay eggs, with a milk carton filled with a mixture of sugar, vinegar, banana peel and water.

Pets in the garden

- If you see bitches urinate on the lawn, pour a bucket of water over the place immediately. This dilutes the urine and prevents it marking the grass, and also gets rid of the scent which would mark that as the place to urinate.

❖ Train your dogs to do their business in a particular place in your garden so you don't have to clear up the whole garden.

❖ Keep pets away from any areas treated with chemicals or tar oil-based products.

❖ Use non-toxic timber preservatives.

❖ Cover slug bait, ant powder and rodent poison so your pets can't get at it.

❖ Provide a patch of soft earth or ashes for a cat toilet and dig it over occasionally to keep it soft and inviting to scratch in.

❖ **Keep a water-pistol handy to discourage your neighbours' cats.** Put some detergent in the water to make sure it sticks to their fur instead of shaking off.

❖ If you are troubled by stray dogs in your garden, get some male human urine and sprinkle it round the boundaries. It will have to be done again after rain, or dogs will assume the territory owner has gone. If applying it from the primary source, make sure no one is about or there may be accusations of indecent exposure.

❖ If using proprietary products to repel animals, avoid getting them on your hands as they can be difficult to get off.

Pets in the garden

❖ Keep cats off your garden by sprinkling a mixture of old coffee grounds and strips of orange peel.

❖ To discourage cats, lay a length of bicycle inner tube on the lawn. The cats will think it's a snake.

❖ To let cats enjoy catnip without destroying the plant, put a wire basket over the plant and let it grow through the mesh.

❖ Plant catnip anywhere you want cats to lurk and discourage birds, such as near your strawberry bed.

Photographs

❖ Over-bright light does not make for good photographs, so take them either early in the morning or late in the afternoon when the light is softer. Cloudy days are the best time to take close-up shots.

❖ Take lots of shots of each subject from different angles and distances, and with different camera settings. If using an automatic camera, use the 'bracket' option to give you three slightly different exposures.

❖ Remember that red is a colour that tends to dominate. If there is a non-essential red item in your composition, adjust your picture to eliminate the red.

- Avoid the difficulties of photographing scenes which include a lot of white flowers by setting the lens aperture half a stop wider than the meter recommendation. This prevents overexposure due to the reflected light.

- Try different shots of the same subject by changing your viewpoint and distance. You don't need a zoom lens for this, just stand closer.

- To alter the emphasis of colours on your composition, try the shot from different angles and against different shades of background. Dark backgrounds tend to lighten colours, light backgrounds tend to darken them.

- Use the artist's rule of 'thirds' to compose good pictures. If your picture was divided into thirds, both vertically and horizontally, the main subject should be at a point where the dividing lines intersect, rather than in the very centre.

- Try photographing plants from unusual angles, for instance you could emphasise the height of a delphinium by photographing it from low down so that it towers above the camera against a clear sky.

- Use natural frames such as gateways or arches to frame your shots.

- Assemble a kit of equipment to enhance the photographic qualities of plants. Professional photographers carry sponges to clean leaves, little pieces of wire and string to relocate leaves and branches, secateurs to remove unsightly dead bits, and a spray of water and glycerine to put a shine on fruit. Some even apply boot polish to root vegetables to make them look better! Obviously you should ask permission before pruning plants in other people's gardens.

❖ Keep a record of every shot you take, noting the date and time, weather conditions, camera settings and details of the location and the plants.

❖ If you have built up a collection of professional quality transparencies, find out if a photographic library would be interested in them. You lodge the pictures with the library and receive a fee every time they are used. This could build up into a nice little income.

Ponds and other water features

❖ To clear the algae and blanket weed from ponds, put a handful of barley straw in a net and hang it in the water.

❖ Make holes in any thick ice which forms on garden ponds, or the gases produced by the pond plants will build up to a toxic level. But don't break the ice by hitting it, or the shock waves could kill your fish. The best method is to fill a plastic bottle with hot water, tie a string to it for easy recovery, and put it on top of the ice to melt through.

- ❖ Site your pond where it will get plenty of light. Water plants need light to grow well, and half the pleasure of a pond is watching the reflections on the water.

- ❖ Always stock a pond with fish. They will eat the mosquito eggs which will otherwise hatch out to bite you.

- ❖ Buy the best quality pond-liner sheet for a longer trouble-free pond life. Cheaper liners may only last a few years.

- ❖ Buy your pond plants from a specialist supplier. Most of them offer 'packages' of plants and water snails for different sized ponds.

- ❖ Leave the water and the plants in a new pond to settle for several weeks before introducing fish.

- ❖ Collect rainwater in a butt to top up your pond rather than using tap water. Rainwater is free of minerals which can lead to a fast build-up of algae and weed.

- ❖ If using large pebbles in a pond or water feature, wash them carefully first, as any dust on them will foul the water and take several weeks to clear.

- ❖ Add lights to your pond for a night-time display. For the most spectacular effects, choose underwater lights to go underneath fountains or behind waterfalls.

Ponds and other water features

- Site fountains where the water will fall onto water rather than the leaves of plants. This will give a more satisfying sound.

- Choose a submersible pump to circulate water for waterfalls or to power fountains. Although the actual pump will cost slightly more than a surface pump, it will be cheaper to install and less noisy in use.

- Put the switch for your fountain pump just inside your back door where it is easy to reach. Then you can turn the water off overnight if you want.

- For a water feature in a very small garden, consider a tub pond made from half a barrel.

- To make a small child-safe water feature, place plastic crates upside down on the bottom of a small pond to reach just below the water level, then pile large pebbles on top. Plants will grow up through the pebbles and a small fountain can be added to splash onto the pebbles.

- Make an attractive patio feature with water pouring out of a wall-mounted pipe into a terra cotta pot and overflowing onto pebbles. But empty the pot for winter as it won't survive hard frost.

- Choose brightly-coloured fish for your pond, such as golden orfe or common goldfish. Allow one square foot (0.3 sq m) of pool surface for each fish.

- ❖ Buy fish, snails and other pond-life only from a specialist supplier, and do not put wild creatures into the pond. Some fish and snails will damage or kill your pond plants.

- ❖ Make a staircase waterfall between two ponds with a sequence of concrete drainage pipes laid horizontally.

- ❖ Make your own tiered fountain with plastic flowerpots and saucers. Put a large saucer at the bottom, with a large pot on it upside down, then a medium saucer and pot, then a small saucer and pot. Drill holes in the saucers to bolt the whole thing together, add a small pump and a bell fountain attachment and watch the water fall from the top down the levels.

- ❖ Beg a plastic mushroom tray from your greengrocer to use for pond plants.

- ❖ If you hope to attract dragonflies to your pond, provide upright marginal plants for their larvae to climb.

- ❖ When removing weed from ponds, put it in a bucket of water for a while to let any small creatures swim out before you throw the weed onto the compost heap.

- ❖ Use your old doormat as a floating 'island' of marginal plants whose roots will grow through the mat into the water. Irises and calthas are particularly suitable for this treatment.

Pot-pourri

❖ Make your own pot-pourri. On a warm dry day, collect rose petals, lavender, honeysuckle, rosemary and any other strongly scented flowers, put them on a tray in the sun and cover with common salt, turning them daily until dry, which usually takes a fortnight. Put in jars with 1 oz (30g) of mixed dry spice, and shake well.

❖ For long-lasting pot-pourri, you need to add fixatives and essential oils. For each four cups of dried petals, mix 1-½ teaspoonfuls each of orris root powder and cinnamon powder, 5 cloves, 6 drops of rose oil and 2 drops of lavender oil.

❖ Top up old mixtures with more petals and fixatives as needed.

❖ Eke out scented petals with brightly-coloured petals, dried citrus fruit peel and small cones from trees such as alder.

❖ For a lavender and rose pot-pourri, mix six cups each of lavender flowers and rose petals with two teaspoonfuls each of cloves, chopped lemon peel and allspice. Add dried flowers such as statice and larkspur for colour.

❖ Make a 'sunshine' pot-pourri with flowers and petals in yellow and gold colours and add lemon and orange peel.

Potting and other composts

❖ Put a handful of plastic packaging 'peanuts' or 'chips' in the bottom of pots for drainage. They weigh less and keep the compost more open than clay crocks.

❖ Sterilise earth from your garden to make your own potting composts by giving it two hours in an ordinary oven at 400°F/200°C or 5 minutes in a microwave oven on full power.

❖ Layer your compost in pots and avoid root disturbance. If you are planting seeds in the pot in which the mature plant will live, fill the pot to within an inch of the top with potting compost, then top it up with seed compost and sow the seeds in that.

❖ Speed germination of seeds by keeping the compost in a warm place, rather than an icy shed.

❖ When flower arranging 'oasis' has broken up too much to use again, crumble it up and add to potting compost to hold water in the pots.

❖ **The loft insulation material Micafil is a good substitute for the more expensive horticultural vermiculite.** Use either as a rooting compost on its own, or use them to eke out your other composts by mixing 1 part vermiculite/Micafil to 3 parts compost. It also helps retain moisture in the compost. For hanging baskets, use a 50/50 mix, but remember to feed the plants regularly as this material has no nutrient value.

❖ Make your own compost blocker with a piece of 3" (8cm) pipe and an old flat-bottomed wine bottle. Place the pipe on a flat surface, fill it with damp compost and ram the compost down with the wine bottle. As an added refinement, to make an indentation for locating seeds, put a bottle top on the middle of the compost before using the bottle.

❖ For the best results from coir compost, mix in some controlled release fertiliser granules before use, and always water sparingly. Ideally, stand your pots on wet capillary matting and let the compost take up what water it needs.

❖ Worm casts are rich in nutrients, making a valuable addition to potting and seed composts, so collect them in the autumn when they are most prolific and store them in a dry place till spring.

❖ To stop compost falling through the holes in the bottom of pots, cut a circle of kitchen paper and put it in before the compost. By the time it has degraded, the compost will have formed a solid enough mass to stay in the pot without further help.

Pressed flowers

❖ Use pressed flowers to make pictures, greetings cards, bookmarks, or to decorate picture-frames.

- ❖ Dress up plain candles with pressed flowers. Press each flower onto the candle and paint over it with a thin layer of melted wax.

- ❖ Make calenders with appropriate pressed flowers for each month.

- ❖ Make personal greetings cards with flowers appropriate to the season.

- ❖ Press flowers immediately after picking. Layer them in tissue paper or blotting-paper, with newspaper between the layers before putting them into the press.

- ❖ Change the newspaper between the layers of tissued flowers every day for the first week. After that, check them every couple of days to ensure there is no more dampness.

- ❖ Once the flowers are dry, store them, still in their tissue-paper, between layers of corrugated cardboard, until you are ready to use them.

- ❖ As a cheap alternative to an expensive flower press, use a stack of telephone directories or other heavy books.

- ❖ Leave plenty of room between each item so they do not stick together when they are pressed.

- ❖ Skeletonise leaves by soaking them in rainwater for three or four weeks before rinsing them and picking off any remaining leaf tissue. Hang them up by the stalk to dry, then flatten them with a cool iron.

Propagating

❖ Take cuttings early in the morning or on a dull day and keep them wrapped in wet newspaper in the fridge if you can't deal with them straight away.

❖ When preparing root cuttings, always cut them straight across the top and slanting across the bottom, so you know which way is up.

❖ Use coloured wool to mark plants you want to keep for seed or cuttings.

❖ Collect your own seed from non-hybrid plants.

❖ Divide dahlia tubers in spring, ensuring that each piece has several buds and at least one undamaged tuber. Plant several in a box of moist peat and sand, then move them into individual pots when they are growing strongly and harden them off to plant outside when all danger of frost is past.

❖ Increase your stocks of herbaceous perennials by dividing them in spring. Dig up the whole plant, insert two forks back to back in the middle and lever the root mass apart. Do this again with each piece, then trim away the dead sections before replanting.

❖ Get the seeds from fleshy fruit or berries by crushing the fruit gently, then soaking them in a bowl of water for several days. Most of the pulp will float off, and you can then rinse the rest off under running water before spreading the seeds out to dry for storage.

❖ Take basal cuttings from chrysanthemums, coreopsis, dahlias, delphiniums, lupins and pelargoniums. To take these cuttings, dig up the plant in late autumn, cut back the stems to 12" (30cm) before planting them in boxes for the winter. When they start to shoot from the base in spring, cut away 3" (8cm) shoots and put them in moist cutting compost until they have rooted and can be hardened off and planted out.

❖ Layer border carnations in summer. Choose long shoots close to the ground, find a point halfway along the shoot and make a sloping 1" (2cm) cut along the stem before pegging this part of the stem down to the soil. Draw some soil over the stem and wait for at least four weeks for roots to form before severing the shoot from the parent plant. Alternatively, peg the stem down into a pot of compost.

❖ Take cuttings of pinks in July, when they will root without heat. Choose stocky young shoots and cut them across a node, then remove the lower leaves before dipping them in rooting powder and inserting them in the compost.

❖ Divide your hostas every other year. As long as each piece has at least three shoots, it can go back in the border, but smaller pieces are best kept in pots until they have bulked up.

❖ Select double-flowered stocks at the seedling stage by leaf colour. Single-flowered plants have dark green leaves, double plants have light green leaves. The different shades are more easily distinguished if the seed-tray is kept at a temperature of 45-50°F/7-10°C.

❖ To increase your stock of heathers, spread the plant from the middle and fill in the gap with an equal mixture of peat and soil. Then pull individual stems back upright through the mixture and wait until they have rooted before severing them from the parent plant. This may take up to 12 months.

❖ Increase your stock of canna lilies by dividing the rhizomes in spring when they have started into growth. Make sure each section has a shoot and roots.

❖ Increase your stock of perennial violas by potting up the cuttings produced when you trim them back in the autumn. Short, soft tip cuttings take readily with warmth below.

❖ To grow the delightful pasque flower (*Pulsatilla vulgaris*), from seed, you have to sow the seed as soon as it is ripe, so start by buying plants, then putting the seeds in a limey compost and waiting until the following year to plant out the seedlings.

- Check round your hellebores in spring for self-sown seedlings and move them to a pot to grow on. If you have different coloured specimens growing close together, the seedlings may be different colours, so it's worth keeping them in pots or a nursery bed until they flower.

- Increase your stock of hyacinths and crown imperials by cutting a cross in the base plate of the bulb before planting. Plant the bulb in the normal way. Leave it until it has finished flowering and the leaves have died down completely, then dig it up carefully and remove the bulbils which will have formed in the cuts. Plant these in trays to grow on to flowering size in three to four years.

- Increase your stock of gladioli by removing the baby cormlets which form under the parent bulb, and growing them in a nursery bed until they are big enough to flower.

- Increase your stock of lilies by removing scales from the bulbs and keeping them in moist peat until small bulbs form. You can also plant the little bulbils which form where the leaves meet the stem.

- Propagate the alpine plants *Lewisia cotyledon* and *Gentiana acaulis* from seed taken from your own plants, but do it immediately as the seeds won't germinate if they are allowed to dry out.

- Propagate camellias by taking leaf bud cuttings

in August. Cut a long shoot into several cuttings, each cut just above a bud, then pare off a sliver of bark from the bottom end before dipping in hormone rooting powder and inserting them into cutting compost.

❖ For a higher success rate when taking box cuttings, take them as heeled cuttings.

Pruning

❖ Keep the best of your shrub prunings for use in flower arrangements.

❖ Wear gloves and keep your arms covered when pruning spurges (*Euphorbia*), as the sap contains skin irritants.

❖ For large stems, or arthritic hands, buy a ratchet pruner.

❖ Keep your pruning tools sharp. Blunt tools tear instead of cutting, leaving messy wounds which can attract pests.

❖ After removing large branches, leave the wound to dry before painting it with wound sealer. Moisture sealed in by painting too soon can encourage decay.

❖ Unless you are dealing with a topiary subject, whatever the specific needs of the plant you are pruning, always prune so that the centre of the plant is exposed to light and air.

- Before pruning apple trees, check whether they fruit from spurs or tips, and prune accordingly.

- For a bumper crop of rose flowers all summer, try the French pruning method. As soon as all the flowers on a stem are finished, prune the stem back to one third of its length, just above an outward-facing bud.

- Prune your roses with a hedge trimmer. Experiments show that this gives a good crop of flowers the following year. This method should work for a couple of years before you need to do a more scientific prune to cut away spindly growth and crossed branches.

- Prune climbing roses in late winter. They produce flower buds all through the growing season, so you won't prevent them flowering with a winter pruning.

- Prune rambling roses as soon as the flowers have finished. They flower on last year's growth, so if you prune them in winter you may remove next year's chance of flowering.

- If you have chosen a species rose such as *Rosa moyesii* 'Geranium' for its decorative hips as well as its flowers, prune it in early spring.

Raised beds

- Mix in plenty of grit with the soil to ensure good drainage.

- ❖ The best and longest-lasting edges for raised beds are old railway sleepers, as long as you want straight edges. Alternatives are scaffold boards pressure-treated with a wood preservative.

- ❖ For other shapes of raised bed, use rolls of half-log pieces, or investigate the possibilities at a good builders' merchants among the ceramic and cement pipes, drain-edging, or curbstones.

- ❖ Make your raised beds no wider than allows you to reach into the centre without having to tread on the bed. This means the soil doesn't get compressed, and also avoids the edges bursting.

Removing large trees

- ❖ Make sure there is no preservation order on the tree by checking with your local council.

- ❖ Unless you are experienced yourself, employ a firm of proper tree surgeons. They may seem to be expensive, but cheaper firms may do expensive damage through inexperience.

- ❖ Make sure the stump and all the roots are removed or you will invite an infestation of fungus which will spread to other trees and shrubs.

- ❖ Consider whether you need to remove the whole tree, or whether removing all the branches and the top of the trunk would leave an attractive stump to use as a training post for climbers.

❖ Ensure that your chosen tree surgeons have adequate insurance to cover accidental damage to your neighbours' property as well as your own.

Root vegetables

❖ **To beat carrot fly, grow carrots in alternate rows with onions.** The scent of onions will mask the scent of carrots which attracts the carrot fly.

❖ **Sprinkle coffee grounds alongside carrots. This is thought to deter the carrot fly.**

❖ When planting potatoes, get best value from your compost by putting it above the seed-potato. The new tubers form above the seed, and very little root goes down below it, so compost underneath is wasted.

❖ Save some potato tubers to plant in June, and you'll have new potatoes again in September.

❖ Instead of going to the trouble of growing new potatoes in the greenhouse for Christmas, grow the old main crop variety 'Pink Fir Apple.' They will keep until Christmas, and have the taste and texture of new potatoes.

❖ Choose blight-resistant varieties of potato, such as 'Sante,' 'Romano,' 'Cara' or 'Pentland Squire.'

❖ Keep bonfire ash away from potatoes. It makes their skin scabby.

❖ To get your own seed from carrots and parsnips

without having a whole row occupied while the plants flower and seed, just save a few of the best specimens from your harvest and plant them out in early March, with their tops flush with the top of the soil. They will flower in late July. When the seed-heads have turned yellow, cut them and hang them upside down in a paper bag until all the seeds have dropped out.

❖ Grow Jerusalem artichokes as a summer windbreak, then enjoy their tasty tubers in the winter. Choose one of the less knobbly varieties, such as 'New White' or 'Fuseau' for easier peeling.

❖ Grow horseradish in an old dustbin to get straight roots and prevent it taking over the whole garden. Just make some drainage holes in the bottom of the bin, fill it with compost from spent growbags, and plant the horseradish in the top. You should have usable roots within a year.

❖ To chit potatoes, save space by stringing them on a piece of thin wire and hanging the wire up in a frost-free shed. A 3' (1m) length of wire will hold about 20 seed-potatoes.

❖ Give your potatoes a coloured mulch. Trials in America showed that yields could be increased by 15 per cent by mulching the plants with white, pale blue, or blue and orange striped straw.

❖ Mix the seed of carrots with that of annual flowers and grow them together in your borders. Their feathery foliage will complement the flowers, and they will be ready to harvest when the flowers die down in autumn.

❖ 'Prune' your potatoes before they flower, cutting them down to 12" (30cm) high, then let the haulms die back as usual. You should get much larger tubers.

❖ Sow carrots before the end of April or after 15th June to prevent carrot fly damage.

Roses

❖ Grow the species rose *Rosa serica pteracantha* on the west side of your garden so you get the full effect of its enormous translucent red thorns in the late afternoon. Prune it hard every year as the thorns are best on the young shoots.

❖ For repeat flowering at high level, choose climbing roses rather than rambling roses which only flower once a year.

❖ When choosing roses to train up against a wall, consider how the flowers will look against the material of the wall. Bright pink roses and red bricks can clash badly, so in this situation it is usually better to choose white, cream or yellow roses.

❖ Always plant roses in a fresh site to avoid rose sickness which strikes when new roses are planted where the old ones were. Alternatively, replace all the soil in your rose beds.

- Take cuttings from your roses in August or September, using ripe wood. Cut it into 4" (10cm) lengths, cutting just above a leaf, then put them in John Innes No 2 compost. Keep the compost moist and leave them undisturbed until the second spring, when they can be transplanted.

- Keep an eye out for outbreaks of powdery mildew and spray with a fungicide as soon as you see it. If left, it will produce spores and start again next year. Choose varieties which are resistant to mildew.

- **_Bury banana skins under your roses. They provide a range of useful nutrients._**

- Distinguish rose suckers by counting the leaves. True roses have five leaves to a stalk, suckers have seven.

- Remove suckers from roses by scraping the soil back and pulling them off. Cutting them will only encourage more to grow.

- Keep indoor miniature roses healthy by standing the pot on a tray of damp pebbles. After they've finished flowering, plant them in the garden and repot them with John Innes No 2 compost before bringing them indoors next year.

- To enjoy the flower forms and strong scents of old-fashioned roses combined with a long flowering season, try the English shrub roses.

- Keep your roses healthy by removing all the dead leaves from under the bushes. This helps prevent black spot and powdery mildew.

- For the strongest roses, buy them as bare-root plants. The smaller plants tend to be the ones that get put in containers.

Safety in the garden

- Always wear gloves when handling bamboo, to avoid tiny slivers of material cutting your hands and getting under the skin.

- Fit nylon blades to your hover mower. They cut the grass just as well as steel blades, but are less likely to damage the mower cable—or your feet!

- Always wear stout shoes or boots when digging or using power tools such as rotavators or mowers.

- Keep a bucket of water handy when you light bonfires.

- Never use petrol to start bonfires. Use paraffin if you must, but fire-lighters are better.

- Invest in a circuit-breaker for electrical tools in case of cable damage.

- Spray on windless days only.

- Wear goggles when operating power tools to prevent flying debris damaging your eyes.

Safety in the garden

- If gardening on an allotment, keep a supply of clean water handy for rinsing off any chemicals which splash onto your skin, and keep a basic first aid kit in your shed.

- Wear long trousers when operating hover mowers. If the blades hit a stone it will be flung out sideways with dangerous force.

- Remove watches, bracelets, and rings before using compost shredders. If a branch is caught on any of these, it could drag your hand into the blades.

- Read the instructions on chemicals carefully and never exceed the recommended strengths.

- Put old tennis balls or other blunt items on top of canes and support sticks to protect your eyes when you bend.

- Switch off all gas-driven machines before fuelling.

- Use a professional electrician to install, or check your own installation of, electrical supplies in your garden.

- When using electrical tools, drape the cable over your shoulder to keep it away from your feet and from the blades.

- Don't pull power mowers towards you when walking backwards. If you slip and fall you could end up mowing your legs!

- ❖ Always wear gloves when handling weed killers and insecticides. Wash your hands and face well after using them.

- ❖ Store weed killers, insecticides and fertilisers out of the reach of children. Never decant any of these items into old drinks bottles.

Salad crops

- ❖ For autumn and early winter salad crops, sow chicory, endive and lamb's lettuce in August and plant them out in the space created by harvesting other crops.

- ❖ If you don't have much space, grow salad crops in tubs on your patio or outside your back door.

- ❖ For the earliest salad crop, try the miner's lettuce, *Claytonia* (now *Montia perfoliata*). Sow it out of doors in late July, or indoors in September.

- ❖ Sow salad seeds in small quantities at regular intervals to ensure a succession of pickings rather than a glut.

- ❖ Make up your own mixture for 'cut and come again' salad. Choose fast germinating plants, such as lettuce, rocket, spinach and any of the oriental brassicas such as pak choi, mizuna greens and loose leaf Chinese cabbage.

- ❖ To force chicory, pot up the roots in autumn and trim the tops down to within 1" (2cm) of the

Salad crops

crown. Invert another pot on top and cover the hole to exclude light. Keep it at a temperature of 50°F/10°C for three weeks, when the chicons should be ready to eat.

❖ Use lukewarm water when watering cucumbers and tomatoes. As they come from hot countries, they prefer warm water and will reward you with an increased yield.

❖ Twist off the leaves of beetroot when harvesting, as cutting makes the beets bleed and dry out.

❖ **To produce crunchy beansprouts, you have to keep them under pressure,** so fit a cover to rest on top of the beans in your sprouter and rest something heavy on top.

❖ Make your own seed sprouter from a plastic tub or large yoghurt pot with some holes punched in the bottom. Use the lid as a drip-tray.

❖ For a delicate flavoured addition to salads, blanch the leaves of salsify and scorzonera by putting a pot over them for two weeks before cutting.

❖ Grow looseleaf lettuces such as 'Oakleaf' or 'Salad Bowl' instead of the hearting varieties. They are less likely to bolt in hot weather, germinate more easily, and often taste better.

❖ When transplanting lettuce seedlings, cut off 1" (2cm) of the main root. This encourages them to heart up well.

❖ When your radishes run up to seed, let them go and add the young seed pods to salads.

Scented plants

These are the easiest to grow and most popular scented flowering plants. Try them yourself: broom, daphne, freesia, gardenia, honeysuckle, hyacinth, jasmine, lavender, lilac, lilies, narcissus, nicotiana, philadelphus, pinks, primula, rose, stephanotis, stocks, sweet pea, sweet rocket, sweet William, verbena, viburnum, viola, wallflower, winter sweet.

❖ Before buying scented roses, visit the grower's nursery at flowering time. Rose scents can vary tremendously and you may find you prefer some scents to others.

❖ Stick to the old-fashioned single-flowered forms of mock orange (*Philadelphus*), as the double-flowered or golden-leaved varieties tend to have less scent. One of the best varieties for scent is 'Virginal.'

❖ Grow a selection of mints, including the white variegated pineapple mint, and the purple-leaved eau-de-Cologne mint.

❖ Choose a sheltered spot for your scented plants, where the fragrances will linger instead of being carried away by the wind.

❖ Lash out on several bulbs of the regal lily (*Lilium regale*) to fill your garden with its heady scent. It needs well-drained soil, or can be grown in pots.

❖ Nip off the stigmas of lily flowers to make them last longer. Keep the pollen away from your clothes as the pollen stains and won't wash out.

❖ Choose the early-flowering *Magnolia stellata*. It is less prone to frost-damage than other varieties, and has lemon-scented leaves as well as fragrant flowers.

❖ Plant scented shrubs such as rosemary, lavender or myrtle (*Myrtis communis*) where they will release their perfume as you brush past them.

❖ If you have a greenhouse or conservatory for winter protection, grow angels' trumpets (*Datura cornigera syn. Brugmansia knightii*), lemon verbena (*Aloysia triphylla*) and citrus trees, or the chocolate scented *Cosmos astrosanguineus*.

❖ For scent in the conservatory, try night jessamine (*Cestrum nocturnum*), stephanotis (*S. floribunda*) tuberose (*Polianthes tuberosa*), moonflower (*Ipomoea bona-nox*), or some of the tropical orchids.

❖ Make room for the sweet briar rose (*Rosa rubiginosa*). Its flowers are scented. but its true worth is in its apple-scented leaves, which give off even more scent when wet.

❖ For scent in the winter and early spring, grow daphne, viburnums, skimmia and witch hazel (*Hamamelis mollis*).

❖ Make a scented corridor of regular routes round the garden by training scented climbers up and over, as well as lining the corridor with lower growing scented plants.

❖ For a little variety in lily of the valley, try the pink-flowered form 'Rosea'; the variegated-leaved 'Variegata' with yellow stripes throughout the leaves, or 'Hardwick Hall' with gold edges to its leaves.

❖ Plant bearded irises in masses to get the best scent. The apricot flowered hybrid 'Shepherd's Delight' is especially fruity scented.

Seaside gardens

These are the easiest to grow and most popular seaside garden plants. Try them yourself: achilliea, antirrhinum, aster, aubretia, broom, coreopsis, dimorphotheca, eryngium, euphorbia, forget-me-not, forsythia, hardy geranium, hebe, hydrangea, hypericum, iberis, ilex, juniper, kniphofia, lavender, linaria, stock, maple, polygonum, potentilla, pyracantha, rosemary, rudbeckia, salvia, santolina, sempervivum, senecio, spirea, stachys, tamarix, veronica.

❖ Buy young, small trees for your seaside garden. They are less likely to blow over than tall trees which have been grown away from the coast and don't have the root structure to cope with the wind. On extremely windy sites anchor newly planted trees with guy ropes as well as stakes until they have had a couple of years to get used to the prevailing wind.

❖ Protect the plants in seaside gardens by planting a thick hedge or shelter belt of trees to stop salt spray.

❖ Choose hebes as seaside shrubs that offer a variety of flower colour as well as good salt resistance.

❖ Plant native seaside plants—thrift, pinks, sea holly, tamarisk, and grey foliage plants such as senecio or santolina which are resistant to salt.

❖ Take advantage of your coastal location to grow seakale and asparagus. Both originated as coastal plants, and thus thrive in salty air.

❖ Visit some seaside gardens which are open to the public to see what thrives in them before buying plants for your own garden.

Seeds

❖ Mark the plants from which you want to save seed while they are still flowering or you'll forget which they are. A piece of coloured wool is all that is needed.

❖ Save your own seed from non-hybrid flowers and vegetables and reduce your gardening bill. Keep an eye on the seed-heads and tie a paper bag or old stocking over them when they are close to maturity, or you may find they've done their thing before you got there.

❖ Make sure self-saved seed is completely dry before storing it. Silica gel sachets help remove moisture.

❖ Store your seeds in a cool dry place. A garden shed is ideal, as long as rodents can't get at the packets.

❖ Store seeds in herb and spice pots. Many of these pots have perforated inner tops, and thus can be used as seed shakers at sowing time.

❖ Use clear plastic egg-boxes as mini-greenhouses for seeds. Put compost and seeds in the egg compartments, water lightly and shut the lid. Stack the boxes up on a sunny window-sill until the seedlings are well up, then open the lids and harden them off to plant outside or pot on as appropriate.

❖ To get just a few small seeds out of the packet, moisten a matchstick and dip it in. A few seeds will attach themselves to it and leave the rest behind.

❖ **Use tea bags as seed starters.** Just pierce the centre, press a seed in and keep the bag moist until roots appear, then pot it on to a 3" (8cm) pot.

- To sow fine seed like lobelia in little clumps, make a template of paper. Fold the paper like a concertina, make holes with a hole punch, iron the paper flat and put in on the compost before shaking the seeds over it. Tap the paper to make the seeds go through the holes, then shake some fine sand over the paper and tap that through the holes as well so that you can see where the seeds are as well as covering them.

- If your seedlings don't seem to be able to get rid of the seed case, it is probably because they are too dry, so spray them with water until the case drops off.

- To make your seedlings sturdier, brush your hand across them a few times each day. Some commercial growers have machines that do this, since it was proved to work at the University of Georgia.

- Make free starter 'pots' for your marrow, cucumber and pumpkin seeds with a piece of thick turf. Cut the turf into squares, put them grass side down in a tray, make a slit in the middle of each square and slide the seed in before watering well. When the roots come through the turf, just plant the whole thing in its final position.

- **Toilet roll centres make good seed pots for sweet peas.** Stand the centres in a tray, fill them with moist seed compost, and push two or three seeds into each roll.

- To ensure germination of seeds collected from your spring bulbs, store the seed in your refrigerator for a few weeks.

- To germinate Alstroemeria seed, soak them in water for 12 hours, sow them in small pots and keep the pots in a warm place (65-75°F/18-25°C) for four weeks before putting them outside in a cool place.

- Buy your seeds by mail. That way you'll know they are fresh and will germinate better than old seed from shops which may have been kept in unsuitable conditions.

- Order your seed early to take advantage of early order discounts.

- Do complain if you get poor results. Send the seed packet back so they can check the batch. They will give you a refund or replacement, and often some other seeds in compensation.

- For best results, sow all seeds except long rooted vegetables in trays to transplant, rather than straight into the ground. For seeds of plants which resent root disturbance, sow individual seeds in small pots or plug-packs.

- Mix very small seeds with fine silver sand for easier sowing.

- **Add 1 teaspoonful of children's shampoo** to each 2 pints (1 litre) of water for seed-trays. This prevents the formation of a crust on the soil which seedlings can't get through.

❖ Press down the compost in seed-trays with a board to provide a flat surface, or the seeds will accumulate in clumps.

❖ When sowing seeds outside in dry weather, make a furrow and water it thoroughly before sowing the seed.

❖ Don't try to sow lightweight seed like carrot or parsnip out of doors in windy weather, or they could blow away before you can cover them.

❖ Spray seedlings with a fungicide to prevent 'damping off'—the affliction which makes them keel over and die.

❖ Prepare greenhouse-grown seedlings for planting out by hardening them off. This means getting them used to the cooler and windier conditions outdoors by standing them outside for longer periods each day. Alternatively, put them in a cold frame and leave the lid open a little more each day and finally each night.

❖ Sow radishes in the same row as slow-germinating seeds like parsnip. The radishes will be up in five or six days to show you where the row is.

❖ Use square flowerpots. They fit together more neatly in trays, and take up less room than the round ones.

❖ Use waxed paper milk cartons instead of plastic yoghurt pots as cheap plant pots. Being square, the milk cartons are easier to fit together in a tray, and you can easily make drainage holes by cutting off corners.

❖ When sowing seeds in hot weather, give the seed trench a thorough soaking before adding the seeds. They'll germinate quickly from lying on wet earth, and their roots will follow the moisture down. It doesn't matter if the soil you cover them with is dry, and the fact that you haven't wet it means that it won't form a crust to impede the seedling's route to the sun. Water again when the seedlings are showing.

Selling your house?

❖ **Grow yellow flowers in the front garden.** This catches the eye of buyers and encourages them to buy, according to colour psychologists.

❖ Fill your house with vases of flowers, especially scented ones such as sweet peas.

❖ If doing major work to tidy your garden up for sale, stick to the old favourites—a lawn for children to play on, hard paths, good-sized patios, well-known plants and shrubs.

❖ Keep lawns neatly edged. This one feature can make all the difference to the look of the whole garden.

❖ If you intend to take any of the plants with you, say so, both when buyers inspect and when instructing your solicitor. If you don't mention it, the buyers are entitled to expect the garden to be as they saw it.

Shady areas

These are the easiest to grow and most popular shade plants. Try them yourself: anemone, aquilegia, astilbe, cyclamen, dead nettle, ferns, foxglove, hellebore, heuchera, hosta, hypericum, lilies, mahonia, oxalis, periwinkle, polygonatum, primula, pulmonaria, rhododendron, trillium, viola.

❖ For semi-shaded borders, try lily of the valley, foxglove, spurges (*Euphorbia*), fuchsias, hellebores, nicotiana, pieris, Solomon's seal, or flowering currants (*Ribes*).

❖ For shady walls, try the variegated form of ivy (*Hedera*), or the climbing hydrangea (*H. petiolaris*).

❖ For summer ground-cover in moister areas, choose from the many varieties of hosta—but watch out for slugs.

❖ Grow bamboos in shady areas, but restrict their roots or they could take over.

❖ If you have shady areas which are also moist, take the opportunity to grow *candelabra primulas* and ferns.

❖ Consider the effect of fallen leaves from shade-producing trees on the plants below. Large leaves from trees such as maples can smother and kill small plants underneath.

❖ Plant early-flowering bulbs under deciduous trees, where they will get sunlight before the tree is in full leaf. Make sure the bulbs get plenty of water until their leaves die back six to eight weeks after flowering.

❖ Choose decorative forms of elder (*Sambucus nigra*) on the edge of shaded areas. This is where the wild form grows naturally in woodland, but you can choose from yellow-, purple-, or variegated-leaved varieties.

❖ To create a shady area where you don't have room for big trees, try hazel or cob-nut bushes. They will produce good shade in four to five years, and will also keep you supplied with useful sticks. As well as the green and purple-leaved versions, there is the fascinating corkscrew version (*Corydalis avellana contorta*) beloved of flower arrangers.

❖ If shade trees are stealing the water and nutrients from your favourite plants, consider excavating a hole and lining it with a thick butyl pond-liner before replanting the ornamentals. Don't forget to make some drainage holes on the side away from the trees.

Sheds

- Look for 'ex-demo' sheds. These are a bargain, not only because of their price, but also because any shrinkage will have been dealt with.

- Choose a shed made of minimal-shrinkage material such as cedar; or one made of UPVC or metal.

- If you intend to keep machinery such as rotavators in your shed, buy one with a wide door.

- If you want an extra-large shed, check that you do not need planning permission for it.

- Fit as many shelves as you can cram in—you'll be amazed how they fill up.

- Fit a shelf under the window for pots of seedlings.

- Add some battens to the edges of the roof to prevent strong winds ripping the tar-paper.

- Put an old metal filing cabinet in your shed as a rat-proof seed store and child-proof chemical-store.

- Make the most of the space in your shed by fixing jam jar lids to the underside of the shelves. All sorts of small items, including seeds, can then be kept in the jars which you just screw to their lids in the usual way.

- Fit a burglar alarm to your shed. Garden sheds are now a prime target for thieves.

- ❖ Fit door hinges and padlock hasp and staples so that the screws are not visible and can't be removed easily by thieves.

Shrubs

- ❖ Shrubs grown for their decorative foliage should be pruned every year to improve the quality of their leaves. Young leaves are better coloured and often more luxurious than older leaves.

- ❖ If you like brooms, choose the Mount Etna broom (*Genista aetnensis*). It lasts many more years than other brooms, and has an upright habit which does not create much shade so you can plant other things underneath it.

- ❖ Plant winter-flowering shrubs where they won't get the morning sun, as sunlight on overnight frost will damage the flowers.

- ❖ Grow wintersweet (*Chimonanthus praecox*) against a sheltered wall and cut flowering sprigs in January to perfume your sitting-room. Grow a flowering climber through it to disguise its dull summer foliage.

- ❖ To get blue flowers on hydrangeas you need aluminium, not iron, so instead of burying old nails underneath the bushes, feed them with aluminium sulphate, sold in garden centres as 'blueing' powder.

- Try under planting your heathers with early-flowering species of tulips such as *Tulipa kaufmania* which opens out into pale yellow star shapes that look best against pink or lilac heathers.

- Make sure you buy a male tassel bush (*Garrya elliptica*) as the catkins on the females are much shorter than on the male.

Sink gardens

- Disguise glazed sinks as stone troughs by spreading on a bonding agent, then pressing on a stiff paste of equal parts of peat, sand and cement. Let it dry for a week before planting.

- Create a miniature rock garden with a lump of soft limestone tufa. Chisel out holes for dwarf plants or small clump-formers like miniature saxifrages.

- When filling sinks, take the compost up to within 2" (5cm) of the top, add the plants and finish off with a layer of gravel to prevent mud-splashes on the plants from rain or watering.

- To prevent the compost going sour, use a proprietary compost or make up your own with two parts of fresh loam, one of leaf-mould, and one of sharp sand with a little bonemeal. Garden soil is not suitable for sink gardens.

Snow

- Leave snow on plants unless the weight is pulling branches out of place and likely to cause permanent damage. In general it does no harm and it protects tender shoots from frost.

- Upright branching conifers like Thuja can be badly damaged by snow, so wrap some wire netting round them to hold all the branches in place if heavy snow is threatened.

- Remove snow from garden paths and driveways by shoveling. Salt will wash into the soil and kill your plants.

Storing fruit and vegetables

- Wrap apples in squares of newspaper and place them in boxes so they do not touch each other.

- Store pears uncovered in single layers, so they do not touch each other.

- Check stored fruit at least once a month in case any of them are starting to rot.

- Store root vegetables in boxes of dry sand, sawdust or peat, arranged with a good layer of the dry material between them.

- Ripen green tomatoes by putting one ripe tomato or a ripe apple in the boxes with them. They do not need to be in bright light.

- ❖ Beans and peas retain their flavour as well, if not better, when frozen unblanched.

- ❖ To store beetroot, twist the leaves off, dry the beets off for a couple days, then put them in perforated polythene bags. This keeps them moist enough to stop them shriveling, and airy enough to prevent mildew.

- ❖ Store potatoes in a cool, dark place. They can be stored in dry peat, but an opaque paper sack will do as well. If you leave them in the light they will turn green and become poisonous.

- ❖ Pack basil leaves into a jar with plenty of olive oil.

- ❖ Tie onions into ropes, or knot them into old stockings or tights, and hang them up in a dry, airy place.

- ❖ Dry beans thoroughly by hanging the whole plant up to dry before shelling them, then pack them into jars or plastic bottles. Check them for condensation after a couple of days; if there is any sign of dampness, spread them out on paper to dry a little longer.

- ❖ Store marrows, pumpkins and winter squash unwrapped but not touching each other on shelves.

- ❖ Thread chilli peppers onto thin string with a needle and hang them up to dry in ropes.

- ❖ Dry apples, pears and plums like Grandma did. Core apples and pears, de-stone plums, cut them into rings and dry them on racks in a very cool oven or in the airing cupboard, then pack them into cardboard boxes between layers of waxed paper.

Strawberries

❖ Prepare your growing site with care as you won't be able to do much to it once the plants are in place.

❖ Choose several varieties with different cropping times to give a longer picking season.

❖ For the best crops, plant strawberries no later than mid-September.

❖ Strawberries need plenty of water, but are susceptible to disease when watered from above, so install a low-level watering system such as driplines or perforated hose.

❖ Give your plants a feed of Gromore after they have finished, to build them up for the winter.

❖ Keep an eye out for the grey mould of Botrytis. Take action as soon as you spot any, or you could lose the whole crop.

❖ Solve the twin problems of weed control and mud-splashes by planting through a sheet of black plastic.

❖ To keep summer fruiting varieties strong and help prevent diseases, cut the leaves off after

Strawberries

fruiting to leave the crown clear. Don't do this with perpetual fruiting varieties.

❖ Propagate your own plants from the runners. Either peg these down to the soil or sink a compost filled pot into the soil and peg the runner down into this. Remove any runner that you do not want for propagation purposes.

❖ Prevent perpetual fruiting varieties from fruiting too soon and exhausting themselves by removing any flower buds that appear before June.

❖ Grow your strawberries in a fruit cage, or net them to prevent birds from eating the fruit.

❖ To avoid all the fiddling that you have to do to get a good crop of ordinary strawberries, grow the smaller berried but better flavoured Alpine strawberry. They can be grown from seed, the plants fruit for many years, and they are rarely taken by birds.

❖ Mulch your strawberries with pine needles. They are woodland margin plants, and appreciate the acidity pine needles add to the soil.

❖ Use old fireguards as mini-fruit cages to keep birds off your strawberries.

❖ If you haven't the space to let your strawberry runners root down on the soil, sever them from the parent plant when the first pair of leaves have formed and treat them as ordinary cuttings.

- Grow strawberries in tubs or tower-pots, where they are less vulnerable to attack by slugs. This method also prevents mud splashing on the fruit when it rains. Alternatively, grow them in small growbags on high shelves in a cool greenhouse.

- To get plenty of water to strawberries grown in patio pots, install a perforated 2" (5cm) drain-pipe in the middle of the pot.

- **Polystyrene ceiling tiles make excellent strawberry mats.** They reflect sunlight up onto the fruit, repel slugs, and are easily cut to fit round the plant.

Sweet corn

- For bumper crops, give your sweet corn a feed of nitrogen granules when the tassels have formed on the cobs.

- Test for ripeness by pinching the top of the cob inside its protective leaves. If you can feel a point, it needs longer; if it feels flat across the top, it's ready. This is a better method than opening the covering and puncturing a kernel to check whether the juice is milky, as this latter method exposes the unripe cobs to birds and the spores of smut disease.

- To ensure germination and steady growth, keep your sweet corn seeds and plants warm. If you don't have enough room in the greenhouse to grow the plants until they are at least 4" (10cm) high, plant them out under a plastic drinks bottle 'cloche.'

❖ Try growing the new 'mini' corn varieties and add the immature cobs to salads and stir-fries.

❖ Try growing some ornamental corn varieties for autumn and winter decorations. Treat them exactly the same way as sweet corn, but keep them well away from sweet corn as cross-pollination will spoil the sweet corn.

❖ Plant dwarf beans between your sweet corn plants and let the beans provide the nitrogen the corn needs.

❖ Don't try to germinate your corn in water or damp tissue before you plant it. As soon as the shoot tip detects light, it goes into its next phase of leaf growth and neglects the first stage of making roots.

❖ When picking sweet corn for the kitchen, make it the last job you do before you leave the garden. The sugars in the kernels start to change to starch as soon as you pick it, and the longer you leave it, the tougher it will get.

❖ Start 'supersweet' varieties of sweet corn in pots indoors and transfer them to progressively bigger pots until the weather outside is reliably warm. These gene-enhanced varieties are trickier to grow than the other varieties.

❖ Keep different varieties of sweet corn separated by a barrier such as a row of runner beans. If they cross-pollinate the corn will be tough and not worth eating. For this reason, allotment growers should get together with their neighbouring plot holders and arrange to grow the same variety.

Sweet peas

❖ To speed germination, weaken the tough seed coat by rubbing the seeds between two sheets of medium grade sandpaper.

❖ Try the dwarf varieties 'Patio Mixed,' 'Little Sweet Heart,' or 'Bijou' in window-boxes.

❖ Sweet peas need a good depth of compost to develop a strong root system. Enthusiasts use special tubes to start their seeds—toilet roll centres are free and work just as well.

❖ Pinch out the tips when the third pair of leaves have developed. This encourages more stems to come from the base and makes for a stronger plant. If you do this with sharp scissors or a knife you can pot up the cuttings to make extra plants.

❖ For exhibition quality blooms, pinch out all but one stem and remove all other side-shoots and the tendrils. You will then have to tie the plant to its stick.

❖ Keep picking the blooms, or deadheading them

as the flowers fade, or the plant will stop production.

❖ Plant some sweet peas in with your runner beans to encourage the bees to visit the beans, and to enjoy the scent while picking beans.

❖ Make a traditional sweet pea 'hut' by twisting and plaiting silver birch sticks together. Take six 8' (2.6m) tall sticks with brushy tops and poke them into the ground to form a circle. Twist the tops together and fasten them to make a dome. Then twist the side branches together to make horizontal rungs. Trim off any spare twigs and put one or two plants at the base of each stick.

Thinning

❖ Thin out bunches of dessert grapes with scissors when the young grapes are the size of blackcurrants. Snip out individual grapes to leave a pencil thickness between the remainder.

❖ Restrict melon plants to four fruits. Pinch out the tips of each lateral shoot when five leaves have grown, to encourage the side-shoots the fruit grow on, and pinch out the side-shoots two leaves beyond each fruit.

❖ Wait until after the 'June drop' before thinning apples and pears. Many excess fruitlets will fall off naturally, then you should thin the remainder to one or two fruits per cluster.

- Thin gooseberries in late May by removing every other fruit. These thinnings can be cooked and the rest left to develop into dessert fruit.

- Thin root crops by pulling alternate plants when they are big enough to be eaten as 'fingerlings.'

- Thin flowers such as dahlias, chrysanthemums and roses by removing all but the main bud on each stem. This will give you one big flower instead of several small ones.

- Thin seedlings sown 'in situ' by using an onion hoe rather than by pulling out plants and risking damage to the roots of the remainder.

- Thin young salad crops such as lettuce and spinach by removing alternate plants to the salad bowl. Keep doing this at weekly intervals until there is enough space for the remainder to heart up.

Tomatoes

- No need to go to the trouble of hanging tomato plants up in the greenhouse to ripen in the autumn, or to wrap each tomato in paper. Just put the green tomatoes in a box with one ripe one, or a ripe apple, and the ethylene gas given off by the ripe fruit will encourage the green ones to ripen.

- Train your tomatoes up wigwams like the ones you make for your beans.

❖ Make a frame to support your bush tomatoes to keep the fruit off the ground. The legs should be 12" (30cm) high, the top should be 12" (30cm) wide, and as long as required, made of four pieces of lath. Place the frame in position as soon as the plants have been set out, and let them grow up through the frame.

❖ To get a bumper tomato crop, let one of the side stems grow and train it sideways at an angle. Nip out the other side stems as usual, treating the plant as a two-stemmed cordon.

❖ Support your tall tomatoes with a single piece of string. Tie one end to an overhead wire or frame, and either wrap the other end round the rootball when transplanting, or tie it to the bottom of the stem. Then, as the plant grows, wind the string round the stem to hold it upright.

❖ To give outdoor tomato plants extra roots to suck up moisture, plant them on their side. Before planting, pull off all except the very top pair of leaves, then make a little trench, lay the plant on its side in it and gently bend the tip upwards above the soil as you fill the trench in. It will then form roots all along the underground stem. Put the support stake in place while you remember where the stem is!

❖ Grow greenhouse tomatoes by the 'ring culture' method and avoid the problems of disease build-up in the soil. This method involves placing bottomless rings of whalehide or plastic on a bed of gravel. The ring is filled with compost which can be given additional fertilisers, but water is applied to the gravel only. The tomatoes develop two sets of roots for feeding and taking up water.

❖ If growing indeterminate or cordon varieties, pinch out the side-shoots and pinch out the top two leaves above the top truss of fruit. Bush varieties do not need to be pinched out.

Tools and equipment

❖ Saw off the outside tines of an old fork with a hacksaw, to make a narrow fork to reach in between closely spaced plants in the border.

❖ For a quick supply of plastic-coated wire plant ties, wrap the wire round a thick stick in a spiral, slide it off and cut up the length of the spiral with wire-cutters.

❖ **Use an old ironing board as a potting bench.** The height is adjustable and you can fold it up for storage.

❖ Clean up plastic plant labels by soaking them in a solution of household bleach for 24 hours.

❖ To store canes neatly in the winter, cut the bottoms out of two used food tins, attach these to the shed wall, and just slide the poles through the two tins.

❖ **Mark a set of measurements on the inside edge of your gardening boots with magic marker.** Then you only have to put your foot alongside the row to see where the next seed or plant should go.

❖ Dress up your metal watering-cans by painting them and stenciling flowers on them in a contrasting colour.

❖ When you cut out the old canes from your raspberries after fruiting, keep them to use as pea sticks.

❖ Hold canes steady in plant pots with two pieces of expanded polystyrene. Poke the cane through the pieces and position them with one piece at the bottom of the pot and the other just below the surface of the compost.

❖ Make sure your house insurance covers your garden shed and its contents. Tell your insurance company if you keep power tools in the shed.

❖ Fit a spring clip to your spade scraper and attach it to the spade handle. This means it is always handy.

❖ Old teapots make handy tangle-free string dispensers. Paint them a bright colour so they are easy to see in the garden, put the ball of string in and feed the end out through the spout.

- ❖ Buy the best tools you can afford. They'll last longer and will be better designed, so will do a better job.

- ❖ Clean digging tools after each use and oil them before you put them away at the end of the season. Spades and forks with steel handles should be hung upside down to let moisture run out, as otherwise they can rust from the inside.

- ❖ For easier digging, try continental shafts for your spades and forks. They look like a heavy broom handle, and give more leverage than the usual short shafts.

- ❖ Make sure the head of your Dutch hoe (the sort you push) is set at the correct angle for your height. It should just skim over the surface of the soil rather than dig in.

- ❖ Wear a glove when using secateurs to prevent blisters.

- ❖ Paint the handles of small tools with bright-coloured paint, so you can always see them against earth or foliage.

- ❖ Don't throw away broken spade or fork handles. Trim them down to make a set of different length dibbers.

- ❖ Keep a separate watering-can for weed killers and label it clearly so it doesn't get used for anything else.

Tools and equipment

- Stand wheelbarrows on end when they are not in use to avoid pools of water gathering in them and causing rust.

- Make a measuring rod, to allow easy spacing of transplants, by putting strips of electricians' insulating tape at appropriate intervals round a bamboo cane.

- Sharp hoes and spades work better than blunt ones, so keep a file handy to hone the edges before starting work.

- Use old umbrellas as supports for tall plants. Take off the fabric, open them out and push the stick into the soil.

- **Use an old apple corer to get deep-rooted weeds out of your lawn.**

- Mend damaged hoses with a short length of copper pipe. Cut out the damaged section of hose, warm the ends in hot water and slip them over the pipe, then bind with wire to tighten the join.

- Make your own seed and transplant pots with newspaper and flour-and-water paste. Just tear the paper into strips and paste layers over the base of a bottle, let it dry and slip it off. When the plants are ready to go outside, plant the whole thing as the newspaper will soon disintegrate. Don't be tempted to use paste as most of these now contain antifungicides which will stop your plants growing.

- ❖ Recycle your Christmas tree by using it as a support for peas or other climbing plants.

- ❖ Cut up old tights and stockings to use as plant ties. Slice them diagonally and slip them over your hand onto your wrist until needed.

Topiary

- ❖ Use hawthorn (*Crataegus monogyna*) as a topiary subject, and trim it in late spring after it has flowered.

- ❖ If you have a very tall hedge, convert it into a steam engine or a cottage with door and windows and a chimney on top.

- ❖ **Delight children by creating a topiary dinosaur or elephant.** You'll need four separate plants for the legs (three for a tyrannosaurus' legs and tail) and a frame to support long tails and necks.

- ❖ Start your topiarising by practising with a simple cone shape. Tie three bamboo canes to make a triangular template, fix it round the plant and clip off everything outside it.

- ❖ Shape holly bushes with electric hedge trimmers.

- ❖ Create a corkscrew shape by starting with a tall cone, then trimming it to make a spiral.

- ❖ Choose box, lonicera, or yew for the neatest topiary shapes.

- ❖ Make miniature topiary subjects from rosemary bushes in pots.

- ❖ Make or buy metal frames for the more elaborate shapes.

Traditional cottage gardens

- ❖ For authentic cottage garden paths, add an edging of scallop shells, and beyond them a neat row of low flowering plants such as baby blue eyes (*Nemophila menziesii*), poached egg plant (*Limnanthes douglasii*), or double daisies (*Bellis perennis*).

- ❖ Choose the older type of roses. Hybrid tea roses look far too 'modern' for this type of garden.

- ❖ Underplant your roses with bulbs and low spreading plants such as hardy geraniums, campanula, corydalis, or lady's mantle (*Alchemilla mollis*) for the 'crammed full' look which typifies the cottage garden.

- ❖ Make or buy arches of rustic poles rather than the modern looking trellis or metal versions.

- ❖ Make a scarecrow for your vegetable garden.

- ❖ Use hazel poles rather than bamboo for your runner beans.

- ❖ Mix vegetables and flowers in the same beds by putting the taller vegetables at the back of the beds to form a backdrop for the lower flowers. Choose varieties of vegetables which are decorative in their own right, such as red cabbage or frilly leaved 'Lollo Rosso' lettuce.

❖ Make paths of old-fashioned materials such as bricks, real stone flags, gravel, or pebbles in patterns.

❖ Include some of the dye-plants in your herb section or elsewhere. Alkanet (*Anchusa officinalis*), dyers woodruff (*Asperula inctoria*), dyers broom (*Genista tinctoria*), and pot marigolds (*Calendula officinalis*) are all traditional cottage garden plants.

❖ Don't forget to plant at least one lavender bush—the classic cottage air and cupboard freshener.

❖ Many cottagers kept bees, so use an old-fashioned bee skep as an ornamental focus, and grow flowers which attract bees, such as anise hyssop (*Agastache foeniculum*), borage (*Borago officinalis*), and lemon balm (*Melissa officinalis*).

❖ Add the finishing touch to the front garden with a piece of topiary. Peacocks are the traditional cottage dweller's choice.

Trees

❖ Protect your privacy from prying neighbours without having the expense of erecting a fence, by planting a couple of trees where they block the sight line from the neighbours' windows to your favourite places.

❖ Encourage sap flow in early spring by beating your trees with rolled up newspapers.

❖ Give your conifers a shake every month to free them of dust and old leaves.

❖ Save the bigger pieces of prunings from your trees and shrubs for use on your barbecue. Fruit wood and herb prunings add a delicious scent to the food.

❖ For a triple value tree, choose the shadberry (*Amelancier canadensis*). Its mature height is about 10' (3m), so it won't crowd a small garden, and it will be covered in white blossom in April, edible black berries in June, and red foliage in autumn.

❖ Resist the urge to plant a weeping willow unless you have a very large garden. They soon become enormous, and have a nasty habit of 'self-pruning'—dropping branches unexpectedly.

❖ Buy shrubs and trees for autumn colour in the autumn, when you can see exactly what colour they will be. Even the most popular ones can come in different strains which may vary in their colouring potential.

❖ Locate holly trees where you won't have to hand-weed. The leaves stay prickly for a long time and can make weeding a painful job.

- Hug your trees to reduce stress and tension. Modern pagans say that deep-rooted trees channel the earth's energy and give it off when hugged.

- Plant flowering cherries at least 30' (10m) away from buildings and walls, as their roots can reach this far and damage the foundations or drains.

- If you have to cut down a laburnum tree, wear gloves, mask and hat, as all parts of the tree are poisonous, and sawdust from the wood is a powerful skin irritant.

- When planting trees in dry or sloping areas, add a 2" (5cm) diameter plastic tube with a couple of inches sticking out, to get water right down to the roots easily.

- If you have birch trees in your garden, under plant them with crocuses for a delightful contrast of colour against the white bark.

- Buy holly trees in pairs. You need both male and female trees if you want berries.

- If you want to grow your Christmas tree on in the garden after the holiday, choose one which has been grown in a container or one which has a proper wrapped rootball. Trees which are sold with bare roots, or which have been potted for sale are unlikely to survive.

- For a permanent Christmas tree, buy a Norway spruce (*Picea abies*) in a pot, and after Christmas, plant it outside, pot and all. You will then be able to dig it up and use it again for several years before it has to be repotted, and will only have to stop doing this when it gets too big to handle or fit in your house.

Trellis

❖ Heighten a fence or wall by adding shallow panels of plain or scalloped trellis.

❖ Create your own designer effects with trellis by painting it white, blue, or green, and adding decorative finials to the posts.

❖ Avoid the cheap expanding trellis. It is too flimsy to fix firmly and doesn't last very long.

❖ Use narrow panels of trellis to make rose arches, pergolas or arbours.

❖ For instant privacy in your garden, nail hessian to trellis panels.

❖ Make your own fashionable planters by attaching a panel of trellis to an oblong wooden trough.

Tunnels and arches

❖ Grow runner beans on tunnels instead of the usual tepees or row of sticks. Set two rows of sticks into the ground, and join them over head-height with bendable hazel sticks. Then walk through the tunnel to pick your beans.

- ❖ When constructing arches for climbing or rambling roses, add wings to the sides to prevent stray branches sprawling over the path.

- ❖ Make your own metal framework with steel reinforcing rod from your local builders' merchant. If you ask them nicely, they'll bend it into shape for you, so all you have to do is set it in place.

- ❖ Create a spectacular laburnum tunnel by planting young trees either side of a path and training the branches to meet above head-height by tying them to bamboo canes.

- ❖ Create a nut tunnel with hazels by tying high branches together across the path.

Vegetables

- ❖ Grow mini-vegetables and say goodbye to leftovers. All you need to do is to plant them closer together than usual and harvest them early. The wide-row system where you grow plants at staggered intervals in blocks is ideal for mini-veg.

- ❖ Use lengths of old hose pipe and bamboo canes to make a crop frame. Just push the ends of the pipe over the canes, stick the canes in the ground, and you have a strong arch to support your net.

- ❖ To hold down your garden fleece, fill old lemonade bottles with water and put a corner of the fleece over the neck before screwing the top on.

Vegetables

- ❖ To make a simple frame to support netting, cut 6" (15cm) lengths of old hose and use these to form right-angled joins between vertical and horizontal poles.

- ❖ To locate seed of old varieties of vegetables, get 'The Vegetable Finder' from The Henry Doubleday Research Centre, Ryton Gardens, Coventry.

- ❖ Wait until root and leaf vegetables are large enough to eat before thinning them, and eat the thinnings as succulent fingerlings instead of composting them.

- ❖ For the best asparagus crops, choose one of the 'all-male' varieties. These give bigger spears much sooner than other varieties.

- ❖ If you are short of space, grow bush marrows instead of the trailing sort. Alternatively, train the trailing sort up tripods or over arches.

- ❖ To perk up soups and stews, try the leaf or 'cutting' celery. It doesn't heart up, but is easy to grow and has a good celery flavour.

- ❖ Give peppers and aubergines shelter from cold winds out of doors, or ideally grow them in a cold-frame or greenhouse.

- ❖ Save your back when sowing large seeds in rows by dropping them down a plastic pipe as you stroll alongside the row.

- Sow radishes with all the seeds that go in the soil rather than in seed-trays. The radishes come up in a few days, showing you where your seed rows are, and effectively thin the rows when you harvest them. This is particularly useful with carrots and parsnips which are slow to germinate.

- If growing greenhouse cucumbers, even the 'all-female' varieties, keep all other members of the cucurbit family well away from them. Cross-pollination from marrow, courgettes, pumpkins or melons will all result in bitter cucumbers.

- Sow a second lot of courgette seeds in July for a September crop when the earlier plants have died back.

- Buy courgette seeds this year to plant next year. Plants grown from old seed produce more female flowers and thus more courgettes, than fresh seed.

Walls

- To make a newly built wall look less 'raw,' and to encourage moss and lichen to grow, paint or spray the wall with a thin solution of manure- or compost-water. Any smell will soon go off.

- If building brick or concrete walls in your garden, be sure to include a damp-proof course to stop water rising by capilliary action. Permanently damp walls tend to develop stained patches and are vulnerable to frost damage.

Walls

❖ Use the sunny side of a solid wall to grow tender plants that might not thrive elsewhere out of doors. In the kitchen garden this could mean figs, grapes, peaches and other tender fruit trees. In the ornamental garden it could help *Fremontodendron* or other tender shrubs.

❖ Brighten up a dull wall with one of the variegated ivies. Ivy does not need any support as it clings to the wall with aerial roots.

❖ Ensure that retaining walls for terraced slopes are substantial enough for the weight of earth behind them. Provide adequate drainage or the wall may collapse after heavy rain.

❖ Avoid growing valerian on or close to walls. It has very strong intrusive roots which can eventually bring the wall down.

❖ Give your house a coat of yellow blossom in the early summer by treating laburnum as a wall shrub. Plant the young trees against the walls, train the branches on horizontal wires, and prune them to keep the growth flat against the wall.

❖ Before planting ivy against brick house walls, check that the bricks do not need repointing. Stop its vertical growth before it gets to the roof, or it could creep under the tiles.

❖ Build a low wall of the type of builders blocks which have square holes in the centre and use these holes as planters.

Watering

- Make a reel to store your hoses by bolting an old car wheel to the shed wall.

- Water outside in the evening, when the sun isn't so hot, so the plants have the night to take up the water before the next day's sun dries it up.

- Water copiously once a week rather than a little bit every day. Sprinkles of water don't penetrate the soil far enough to do any good.

- Spot-water individual plants such as tomatoes or newly planted ornamentals, by sinking a flowerpot into the soil next to them and filling it with water. Alternatively, cut the bottom off a plastic bottle and sink that into the soil with the neck near the roots.

- Tie a broom handle to your hose pipe for watering hanging baskets. Leave 12" (30cm) free at the end to bend naturally.

- Stand tubs or pots of plants underneath your hanging baskets so they benefit from the water dripping from above.

- Lime-hating plants need lime-free water. If your tap water is chalky, save rainwater for these plants, or acidify your tap water with old tea bags.

- When fitting an outside tap for a hose, make sure it has a nonreturn valve. Failing to do this could result in a large fine, as there is a risk of pollutants being sucked into the water system in the event of a sudden drop in mains pressure.

❖ **Put an old sock or stocking over the end of drainpipes** to act as a filter and keep leaves and rubbish out of water butts.

❖ In drought conditions, leave your hoe in the shed and pull weeds by hand. Hoeing breaks up the crusty top layer which protects the moisture lower down in the soil from evaporation.

❖ To keep the ground moist round any favourite shrub or tomatoes, fill a plastic bag with water, tie the neck tightly, tie it to a stick and make a pin-prick hole in the bottom. It should then take several days for the water to seep out. Add liquid manure when necessary.

❖ In the greenhouse, only water the plants that need it. Pick up each pot and feel its weight. If it feels light, water it, if not, don't.

❖ Install as many water butts as you can, linking them so that each one overflows into the next. Stand them up on bricks so that you can easily get a watering-can under the tap.

❖ In drought conditions, divert your bath and kitchen water into water butts. Plants can tolerate soap and a little detergent, but not bleach or salty water from dish-washers.

❖ If you are planning any excavation work in your garden, or returfing your lawn, take the opportunity to install water pipes at strategic points where taps will save your legs. Ideally, you should add drip irrigation or mist watering systems.

❖ When your hose gets old and starts to leak, stop one end with a cork, make some more holes, and use it as a drip waterer.

❖ Let the leaf-shape of your plants tell you how they want to receive water. As a general rule, leaves are shaped and arranged in such a way that they will shed rain where the roots are—for instance, rhubarb channels it down the centre of the leaf into the centre of the plant where it can go down to the long root, while most trees shed water from leaf to leaf until it falls to the ground on the drip-line at the edge of its canopy, which is where the roots are waiting for it.

Weeds

❖ Get rid of broad-leaved weeds in your lawn and feed the grass at the same time by putting a teaspoonful of Growmore in the middle of each weed. The excess fertiliser kills the weed and encourages the grass to grow over the empty patch.

❖ To get weed killer onto weeds in a densely-planted bed, put a hole-free rubber glove on your hand, then an old woollen glove on top. Dip your gloved fingers into the weed killer and stroke it onto individual weeds. Add a little flour to the mixture and you will be able to see those you have done.

❖ Protect precious young plants from hoeing by slipping a length of drainpipe over them.

❖ Kill chickweed by watering it with a solution of 1 measure of Jeyes fluid to 10 of water.

❖ Get rid of couch grass by growing tomatoes where the couch grows. The tomatoes give off a substance that couch grass doesn't like, and it won't come back.

❖ **Mix 1 fl oz (25cl) each of liquid detergent and gin** in 2 pints (1 litre) water, bring to a boil and pour it over weeds on paths and patios.

❖ Lay newspapers on the soil round large plants to prevent weed seeds germinating and starving perennial weeds of light. Wet the newspapers well and cover them with mulching material to disguise them.

❖ Hoe weeds when the sun will kill them before they root down again.

❖ Keep containers at strategic points round the garden to hold weeds and pull a few every time you go out in the garden.

❖ Use eye-brow tweezers to remove weeds from pots and around seedlings.

- ❖ Hoe as soon as weed seedlings appear. The younger they are, the easier they are to deal with.
- ❖ Never walk past a weed. Pull it out before it gets big enough to set seed.
- ❖ Some weeds such as marestail are resistant to weed killer because the leaf structure shrugs off water. Add soft soap to the mix to make it stick to the leaves.
- ❖ Always pick up hoed remains of weeds that are flowering. They will continue to set seed even when they appear dead. Groundsel is notorious for this.
- ❖ **Learn which weeds are edible,** such as young stinging nettles or fat hen, and get some use out of them.

Wild flower gardens

- ❖ Work with nature rather than fighting it. Choose wild plants that would naturally grow in your district and on your type of soil.
- ❖ Get your plants and seeds from specialist suppliers or friends' gardens. It is an offence to take them from the wild.
- ❖ Leave cutting the grass of wild flower 'meadows' until late summer, when the flowers will have shed their seed.
- ❖ Establish a wild flower meadow by raising young plants in pots or plug-packs and then planting

them out. This is much more dependable than sowing seed directly into the meadow. Cowslips are particularly easy to grow from seed.

❖ Avoid take-overs from colonising plants like celandine by restricting their roots.

❖ Where you are growing wild flowers in grass, be sure to remove the clippings when you cut the grass. Wild flowers do best in poor conditions, and grass clippings rot down to nourish the soil.

Wildlife in the garden

❖ Deter mosquitoes from biting you by rubbing a little oil of citronella on your forehead, wrists and ankles. Keep the oil in a glass bottle, as it destroys plastic. It also dissolves the sticky stuff in band-aids plasters, so keep it away from them, unless you want to get them off!

❖ Pile bonfire material in a collection heap and only move it to the fire site when you are ready to light the fire. Setting fire to a pile of material that has been standing for any length of time means you will kill many beneficial insects and could roast a mouse.

❖ **To discourage moles, buy a musical birthday card,** start the tune playing and shove the card down the mole run. The music interferes with their ability to hear worms and beetles, so they go somewhere else to hunt for their supper.

- ❖ ***Ancient Roman gardeners say to locate a wasps' nest, you should tie a length of coloured thread to a wasp's leg and follow it home.***

- ❖ Deter moles by growing caper spurge (*Euphorbia lathyrus*). Its roots produce a substance that moles dislike.

- ❖ Deter moles by watering round their runs with a solution of Jeyes fluid in water.

- ❖ To stop deer invading your garden, hang bars of scented soap along the boundaries.

- ❖ To stop rabbits eating your favourite plants, smear the stems with garlic paste.

- ❖ Get rid of moles by mixing two tablespoonfuls of animal repellent such as 'Scoot' with 1 gallon (4 litres) of water and pouring it down the runs.

- ❖ If you have foxes in your garden, don't use hoof and horn or bonemeal as fertilisers. The foxes will dig it up—and your precious plants with it.

- ❖ To encourage the harmless solitary bee, fix a bundle of hollow sticks in a tree for them to nest in.

- ❖ Lay a sheet of corrugated iron in a rough grassy area to attract lizards, slow-worms and small mammals like woodmice and voles.

- ❖ Ask your local branch of Nature Conservancy for free advice on construction of nesting-boxes for birds, roosting-boxes for bats, and hibernation-boxes for friendly animals.

❖ Encourage butterflies, bumblebees and other insects to visit your garden by growing flowers that provide the nectar they need. Buddleia, Michaelmas daisies, sweet William, sedum and many other common flowers are popular sources of nectar.

❖ **Encourage butterflies to breed in your garden by letting stinging nettles grow in an undisturbed corner.** Many species will lay their eggs on stinging nettles.

❖ Provide a sloping side and marshy fringe to your pond, so amphibians can get in and out easily, and so that useful animals can drink.

❖ To avoid damaging hawkmoth caterpillars, use shears rather than mechanical hedge-trimmers, and don't cut between mid-June and September.

❖ To attract moths, grow honeysuckle, nicotiana, night-scented stock or evening primrose (*Oenothera spp.*), all of which give off moth-attracting scent at night.

❖ To avoid killing bees and butterflies, avoid putting insecticide on open flowers. Alternatively, choose an insecticide which is labeled 'bee-friendly.'

❖ Look for the 'butterfly' and 'bee' marks in seed catalogues when choosing flower seeds.

- ❖ If you have tall trees in your garden, put up boxes for bats to roost in.

- ❖ Make log-piles for wood-boring insects to feed on, and for useful animals to rest under.

Window-boxes

These are the most popular and easiest to grow window-box plants. Try them yourself: daisy, tuberous begonia, pot marigold, celosia, lobelia, night-scented stock, geraniums, pansy, polyanthus, nasturtium.

- ❖ Try an all-white window-box with begonias, pelargoniums, marguerites and white lobelia.

- ❖ Anchor window-boxes to the window-frame with wire or chain, or fit front brackets to prevent them falling.

- ❖ Make your own window-boxes from ordinary planed deal, held together with brass screws. Paint it or treat it with timber preservative but not creosote which is poisonous to plants.

- ❖ Avoid growing lobelia in boxes for upstairs windows. It becomes quite tatty underneath as each batch of flowers dies, and you can see this when you look up from below.

- ❖ Grow evening-scented flowers in your window-boxes and enjoy the fragrance as you sit indoors in the evenings.

- ❖ Choose flower colours for your window-boxes that will not clash with the surrounding material or the curtains inside. Pink flowers and red bricks are particularly likely to clash.

- ❖ Buy several spare troughs to allow you to replace tired displays with fresh ones and change the contents with the seasons.

Wind protection

- ❖ Permeable walls and fences make better windbreaks than solid walls or fences, which can create swirling turbulence on the leeward side.

- ❖ Protect tender plants and newly planted shrubs from cold winter winds with a perforated plastic sack fixed to four canes set in a square round the plant. Alternatively, wrap the plant with hessian and tie it securely.

- ❖ Support young trees with a stake set on the windward side. One third of the stake should be below the ground and the top of the stake should be just below the lowest branches of the tree. Use purpose-made tree ties to tie the stem to the stake.

- ❖ Support herbaceous plants with purpose-made supports or twiggy branches pushed into the ground next to them. Alternatively, use a wire coat-hanger with one end fastened to a bamboo pole.

- ❖ Give Brussels sprouts, sweet corn and giant sunflowers extra help by earthing up the stems.

Winter colour

❖ For a shrub that can be trained up trellis or allowed to cascade in dense mounds, choose the winter jasmine (*Jasminum nudiflorum*). It has no scent, but its little star-like flowers are cheerful on a dull day.

❖ On acid soils, create a carpet of colour by growing a selection of heathers.

❖ If you have room for trees in your garden, choose the ones which have attractive bark to provide interest when the leaves have gone. For instance, Mount Wellington eucalyptus (*E. coccifera*), snake bark maple (*Acer pensylvanicum*), Erman's birch (*Betula emanii*).

❖ In gardens too small for trees, provide winter interest with shrubs which have attractive stems, such as the red-stemmed dogwood (*Cornus alba* 'Sibirica'), corkscrew hazel (*Corylus avellana contorta*), or the white- or yellow-stemmed blackberries (*Rubus cockburnianus*).

Zinnias and other odds and ends

❖ Delight all the flower arrangers you know by growing the green-flowered zinnia (*Z. elegans* 'Envy').

❖ Make a flowering clock from the flowers which open and close at different times of the day. For instance, poppies open first thing in the morning, helianthemum and cistus drop their petals by noon, gazanias open between 10 am and 4 pm, sisyrinchiums open midday, marvel of Peru (*Mirabilis jalapa*) opens at 4 pm.

❖ To prepare loofahs for use in the bathroom, harvest them when they are completely mature and deep gold in colour. Immerse them in water and leave them until the flesh has decomposed, leaving only the woody fibres. Scrub them with a brush, then boil them to get rid of the last of the flesh.

❖ To make walking-sticks from your Jersey Giant cabbages, trim off the roots and growing tips, strip off all the leaves, and wash them with a mild disinfectant to get rid of dirt and organisms that may start them rotting. Leave them in an airy, dry shed for at least 6 months to dry, before smoothing them with sandpaper and varnishing them. Add a rubber ferrule and a wooden knob for the handle.

❖ If you have a new house and the builders have left a thin or rutted layer of topsoil, rake it back and make sure the subsoil is level before you start work. Where the topsoil is really thin, consider buying topsoil rather than battle with what's there.

❖ **Growing plants for love potions?** Use the soil taken from under your foot where you were standing when you heard the first cuckoo of the year.

- ❖ Keep a gardening diary, to keep track of when you sowed and planted, when you harvested; and which seeds and plants were successful.

- ❖ Have fun with a giant sunflower when the petals have gone, by making the seed-head into a face. Use grasses for hair, crab apples for eyes and nose, and bean pods or carrots for a mouth. 'Male' versions might even smoke a pipe.

- ❖ Be kind to your postman—keep prickly plants well away from your front path.

- ❖ **Keep witches out of your garden by growing a rowan tree (Sorbus aucuparia).**

- ❖ Make your scarecrow move. Suspend it from a bent steel pole so that it moves in the wind.

- ❖ To start mosses, ferns, or house-leeks growing on a tiled roof, mix manure and clay into a soft dough, trowel it onto the tiles, and stick the young plants in place with a hairpin. Spray them at intervals during dry weather until they are established, or the whole thing will dry up and blow off.

- ❖ Use a builders' level when installing a sundial. The face must be completely level to function correctly.

- ❖ To clear a badly overgrown garden, get some electric fencing and install a free-ranging pig. On a smaller scale, chickens will do quite a good job, but they won't dig up roots like pigs.

❖ Join your local allotment society as an associate member. This will allow you to buy from their trading outlet at discount prices.

And finally, to halve your workload . . . Marry a keen gardener.

Section II

Garden Tips from America

Lorisa Mock has done a wonderful job in presenting a variety of useful information on gardening. Her vast knowledge of gardening is partly due to the fact that she has maintained gardens in various parts of the U.S., as well as abroad.

If there is something about gardening that was not covered in Section I, there is a very good chance you will find it here. Lorisa has presented an array of gardening insights in a clear and concise manner. Some of the information in this section was compiled by an independent researcher.

Advice

❖ Everyone is an expert and there are as many garden experts as experts in child-rearing. Through trial and error, observation and research, you too can become an expert, so trust your own judgement and you'll enjoy your garden more.

❖ However, for very good advice, soil tests, and lectures, contact your State University County Cooperative Extension office. They'll be listed under County offices. They have agricultural and horticultural agents that can answer your questions about your particular region. Many counties offer the Master Gardener Program that gives excellent gardener training in exchange for volunteer community service.

❖ **Beware of gadgetry.** Claims that a tool will make back-breaking or impossible tasks a breeze are charlatanry, brought to you by the same folks who promised you the free lunch. And remember ... compost happens—you don't need expensive equipment to make it.

Annuals

❖ Use them but don't over use them. They are excellent for providing color all summer. Look for types that self-sow to save work and expense (Cosmos, Cleome, *Verbena bonariensis*, California Poppy, to name a few).

❖ If you don't have the facilities to start off unusual annuals, use the ordinary ones you can find at your local garden center and plant them in surprising colour combinations. A medium size orange marigold, Petunia Purple Wave (it is a ground cover type) with Dusty Miller *(Cineraria senecio)* and a bright red geranium *(pelargonium)* makes a show-stopping and slightly blinding display all summer into the first frosts. Remember that plants you transplant in will still need regular watering because their roots have not had a chance to spread out.

Bulbs

❖ The general rule of thumb is to plant the bulbs 2½ times their depth. Plant in bunches of twelve or so. Plant ten times more than you initially think you need.

❖ Plant **tulips** 9" deep (that means the "nose" of the bulb is that many inches below the surface). This keeps the bulb flowering instead of dividing, and avoids the infamous "collateral damage" caused by your own spade.

❖ Do not put bulb fertilizer directly in the hole when planting. Actually, don't fertilize anything when planting. Instead, apply fertilizer to the soil surface every fall when they are putting on their root growth, and in the late spring when they are storing nutrients for next year.

❖ If the ground freezes in the fall before you've had a chance to plant all the bulbs you ordered, pot them up and keep them in an unheated garage, checking every once in awhile to see that they are still slightly damp. Move them outside when the hard freezes are past. Or bring a few into the house for forcing; the earliest bulbs are best for this.

Buying plants

❖ ***Buyer beware.*** Garden Center staff members are not there to be your friends, they are there to sell you plants. Take your reference books with you, or ask to use theirs: they have them. You want to be sure you can provide the right conditions for your plant. Unscrupulous or uninformed nurseries will sell plants that are not hardy for your region.

❖ Also, the plants you buy from Garden Centers are nitrogen Junkies. They have been pumped up with fertilizer with every watering. So give them a fix at least one or two times a week or plant them with a time-release fertilizer such as Osmocote.

Children in the garden (See also, **Wildlife**)

❖ ***How to encourage them.*** Don't expect them to hoe that row effectively or enthusiastically. Garden tools are not designed for small hands and little bodies. Make forays into the garden instead of marathon work sessions. Save the "fun" jobs for them: planting, weeding the kind of weeds that come out easily, and harvesting strawberries. Devise picnics and other fun activities in the garden. Plant a sunflower "room" or a hyacinth bean (*Dolichos lablab*) teepee.

❖ **How to discourage mess.** Give them their own area to garden (to dig) so you don't lose your precious plants. Help them with simple to grow plants—for example, cosmos, scarlet runner bean, carrots, radishes, anything to ensure instant success and therefore satisfaction. Don't place your favorite plants near walkways or play areas. If you want to keep them out of an area, thorny plants are very useful, and no one likes to walk in groundcovers that are more than six inches high. Make it clear that your time in the garden is necessary for your sanity so they will not begrudge the time (rolling your eyes, frothing at the mouth and twitching uncontrollably should get the message across).

Chrysanthemums

❖ Fall is not the best time to plant mums ... very few plants should be planted while they are in full bloom, after all. Even so, just make sure you plant them as soon as possible, like immediately. Mulch around them for the winter. In the spring cut back the dead. Remember to water during the driest weather. When there are seven pairs of leaves start pinching off the tops to encourage branching. Do this every other week until July 4th weekend and they'll bloom nicely for you again. After several years lift the plant in early spring and divide as the center dies out eventually.

Cut flowers

❖ As an alternative to Ms. Mcdonald's suggestion of putting cut flowers in fizzy lemonade (a 7Up-like drink), make your own floral preservative with a tablespoon of sugar, a tablespoon of lemon, and a teaspoon of bleach per gallon of water.

Design points

❖ Color combinations are a matter of personal preference. If visitors to your garden wince, you might want to change things next season. Make note of combinations you like (they can be texture and form combinations) from other gardens and magazines. Really, write it down, you'll never remember.

❖ Take a **weekly walk** around your garden (well, try at least once a month), making note of what's blooming, what things you want to change or move, and what additions you would like to make. This will make your bulb ordering, for example, much simpler.

- ❖ Don't try **to "hide" an eyesore** in your garden by planting around it ... this actually draws your eye to it. "Ah, what nice hydrangeas around that air conditioning unit." Block the view closer to the observation point, cutting off the angle.

- ❖ When making design changes, think about how you will maintain the garden, i.e. **don't build in problems.** Provide wide paths for frequently traveled areas. Make the openings and gates large enough for wheelbarrows and other equipment.

- ❖ **Benches** are more inviting if they are on the level.

- ❖ Don't plant a narrow bed along the wall of your house. The eaves prevent water from getting to the plants and the concrete foundation leaches into the soil making it too alkaline for most plants. Make a larger bed away from the house that you can view and enjoy from inside.

Digging

- ❖ Digging onto a tarp makes cleaning up on turf so much easier. Always have some extra topsoil on hand when transplanting or planting. Somehow there's always less soil to go back in the hole.

Dried flowers

- ❖ Hunt for naturally dried materials along the roadsides in early summer (don't cause any car accidents). Collect after a couple days of dry weather and make sure they are free of wildlife before you bring them into the house. Don't deplete any source of seed, only take from the wild when there is an abundance.

Easy to grow plants

❖ **Beware of plants** sold as "vigorous" or "easy to grow" plants—these are often very invasive and will take over small gardens, choke out your favorite plants, lift sidewalks, and even steal small children. Conversely, if you have a difficult space you want to fill, plant several vigorous species and let them fight it out.

Evening gardens

❖ Plant white flowers, nicotiana species, and the moon vine where you sit on summer evenings. *Dictamnus albus*, the gas plant, produces volatile oils that can be lit with a match on June evenings—a boon to those with very quiet lives.

Grasses

❖ There are grasses for any condition that your garden can offer; wet, dry, sun and even shade. Excellent books are available. Position your grasses so the late afternoon back-lights them. Grasses are often touted as being low maintenance but do not forget that they will need dividing every few years.

This can be a monumental task with the larger varieties.

Health

❖ Take care of yourself. Lift heavy plants using your leg strength. When digging, don't dig and twist. To avoid prolonged repetitive motion and to pace yourself, vary your tasks by the hour. Remember, this is supposed to be fun.

❖ If **Lyme disease** is a problem in your area don't let it stop you from gardening. As soon as you go in for the day, put all of the clothes you were wearing directly in the washing machine and head for the shower. Ticks can easily be removed before they have a chance to attach themselves, so leave no portion unscrubbed.

❖ **Poison ivy** and **oak** rash can be avoided by the same tactic; starting your shower off with cool water is best. Wear gloves. Wash with a strong soap like Fels Naptha. Clean tools with Murphy Oil Soap to avoid reinfection.

Herbs

❖ To grow **herbs inside**, you will need a cool window with plenty of light. They need excellent drainage, so a gravelly soil mix is best. Clip often to avoid them becoming straggly. Buy healthy, robust plants and plan to have to replace them, so pot them up separately. Basil does not do well in the cold and low light of northern winters, so it's not your fault it didn't grow.

❖ Many of the pungent herbs **repel insects,** so incorporate them in your flower beds, rather than centralizing them into one garden of their own.

❖ Cheer yourself up with an herb tea of fresh thyme or lemon balm. Nursing mothers should not drink tea made of sage. Pregnant women should not drink pennyroyal tea—actually, nobody should, it doesn't taste very good.

Houseplants

❖ Visit your nearest tropical rain forest to understand how many of your houseplants grow in nature.

❖ **Water.** Don't over water them. Don't underwater them. What does this mean? The general rule of thumb is actually a rule of finger .... To tell if the plant needs watering, put your forefinger into the soil mix and if it is dry a ½ inch down, it needs water.

❖ When you water, do it thoroughly. Water should come out the bottom of the pot.

❖ Place saucers under the plant so you won't be inhibited from watering.

❖ Many houseplants are from the tropics. They thrive in low light and humid conditions. You can mist them if your house is very dry (especially with forced air heating) or put a layer of gravel in their saucer and keep water there so the pot is over, but not sitting in, water. The age-old practice of putting crock (broken pottery) or gravel in the bottom of a pot is a load of crock: drainage holes and a soil mix that drains well is sufficient.

❖ Add a little bit of general **fertilizer** (25% recommended strength) to every watering instead of trying to remember to fertilize every month. Do not fertilize an over-dry plant.

❖ **Re-pot plants** when they are pot bound (when you loose the plant from the pot, there are more roots visible than soil). Or when the soil has broken down and doesn't seem to hold air spaces. Leave a space at the top to give room for watering.

❖ Collect **rainwater** for your plants—city water has chlorine and fluoride which can hurt your plants over a long period of time.

❖ Houseplants benefit from an occasional **shower** of tepid water. Leave them under a gentle shower for a generous fifteen minutes and leave them there to drain. Remember to warn your household members—no one wants to be confronted with a jungle in their usually temperate zone bathroom.

- ❖ Move **houseplants outside** to a very shady area after danger of frost. This is best done on a cloudy and windless day. Cover the plants with row covers (agricultural fleece) for the first few days to prevent wind and sun burn. Don't forget to water and fertilize them.

- ❖ Make sure the plants are pest-free before you bring them back in at the end of summer.

Labelling

- ❖ Labelling is very important. Not only does it help you remember a plant's name, but it will remind that it is there. Even professional gardeners have been known to stand on one plant while planting a new one. The three inch white plastic labels can be shoved into the ground so that they are out of sight (leave them in view if you want to create the feeling of a mouse graveyard). Use soft pencil—permanent ink just isn't.

Lawns

- ❖ Be environmentally responsible and don't have a lawn if it requires copious amounts of water or pesticides. Groundcovers and native plants can be used instead.

- ❖ If you aren't trying to maintain a show garden or putting green, you might want to leave the **moss** in your lawn and even encourage it: it doesn't grow high, or require water and it stays green all year round. Equally, clover provides the grass with nitrogen it fixes from the atmosphere.

❖ **Don't fertilize** in spring with a high nitrogen (that's the first number in the three number chemical description) product. It makes for fast, weak growth that attracts pests and needs mowing. Fertilize lightly with a general fertilizer and then fertilize again in the fall two weeks after the last mowing.

❖ **Wildflower** seed mixes don't work.

❖ Wildflower **"meadows"** are not low maintenance gardening. They need selective, informed weeding and annual replanting. Many townships have ordinances on keeping your grass cut to a certain height. However University studies found that neighbors will tolerate a wildflower area in your front yard much better if you keep at least 25% of the total area mowed.

Mulch

❖ Be careful with mulch. If applied too thickly, it can absorb all available rain, causing the roots to come up in search of moisture. Keep mulch away from tree bark and other plant stems.

❖ Mulch your vegetable garden paths with a layer of whole newspapers unopened and over-lapped, topped with a layer of wood chips. This can be tilled into the soil the following spring.

Peonies

❖ To transplant peonies so that you don't miss any seasons of bloom, wait until they have finished flowering, dig them up and shake the soil from the root mass. Allow them to "rest" or cure on the ground in the shade for at least three days and then replant them about 6" below the soil surface. One friend drove around with a peony in her car trunk for two weeks. She planted it and the next spring it bloomed beautifully. A curing period is recommended; the car trip is not necessary!

Pests of houseplants

❖ Generally, spraying your plants with water, as in the shower every month and a **preventative** horticultural oil spray once a month will keep most of the common pests away.

❖ Do not buy infested or infected plants, or even give them house room.

❖ If a plant starts looking really bad, throw it out—they rarely recover and you didn't bring plants into your home to be eyesores. If you want to give it one more chance, cut it back, repot it, put it somewhere out of direct light (preferably out of sight) and see if it comes back. Not all species will respond to this treatment, but it's worth a try.

- ❖ **Whitefly** lay their eggs underneath the leaves. Spray the plant with horticultural oil or insecticidal soap every seven to ten days. Insecticides with pyrethrins (a plant-derived substance) are also effective: follow the instruction on the label.

- ❖ **Aphids** feed on new growth. They can be washed off with a heavy spray of water. Maybe you should do this outside. Or treat them as for whitefly but every 3-5 days.

- ❖ **Scale** crawl all over the plants as youngsters but are invisible. As adults they form a small hard brown shell or scale on the underside of leaves and along the stems. Use insecticidal soap and a green scrubby thing to wash the plant and remove the scales. Spray weekly thereafter.

- ❖ **Mealy bugs** are white armadillo-looking guys that produce cottony deposits which are egg masses. You can kill them with alcohol on a cotton swab, or scrub them off with soap. Be careful, they can hide in the smallest crevices. Simply prune off the badly affected portion. Several bug hunts will have to be staged. Heavy infestation? Seriously evaluate if you need this plant. If the plant is a manageable size, you can invert it (holding onto the soil) into a sinkful of soapy (insecticidal soap) water; swish it gently back and forth to dislodge the pests.

- **Spider mites** are very tiny and live mostly on the underside of the leaves. It will be easier to detect them by their tiny webs. They thrive in hot, dry stressed situations. Wash off with a heavy spray of water. Spray with horticultural soap and stop under watering.

- **Stressed plants** are more likely to get pests and diseases. Think about your plant's welfare. Is there enough light to take a photograph? If not, the plant isn't getting enough energy to thrive. Keep them away from heat sources. Air circulation is important but drafts can be fatal. It's all a balance. If you situate a plant for decorative purposes, instead of considering its needs, be prepared to replace it every three months or so, or consider plastic.

- You can turn an unused corner into a **plant haven** by rigging grow lights and incandescent lights on a simple timer. A small fan will keep the plant healthy if your little display turns into dense undergrowth.

- Above all, do not form an emotional attachment with your plant that would prevent you from disposing of it when it gets unhealthy, or worse yet, ugly.

Plant names

❖ The naming of plants. Most plant catalog companies are in the business for the money, not for informing the public. They dress up many ordinary plants with fancy names and with claims that they are rare and exclusive. It pays to find out what a plant really is ... scientific names are pesky but are more accurate.

Staking

❖ Do it early! Before your plants are flopping over, before that wind storm is brewing on the horizon. It helps to know the potential height of your plant—labelling to remind yourself can help a lot. You probably need stronger support than you think. Use twiggy branches as "pea staking" to support perennials. For larger plants use six to eight bamboo stakes and tie several rows of string looped around. For really large plants, like the grass *Eranthus ravannae*, try reinforcing bars (re bar) cut to 5ft lengths. Taking care of this early means the leaves can grow around and hide the means of support. However, a plant tied too tightly can look a lot worse than one flopped on the ground—at least that looks natural!

❖ Make **plant ties** from old pantyhose cut into strips. They are very strong but stretch to let the plant grow.

Tomatoes

❖ Support your tomatoes with a cylinder or cage made of heavy gauge wire mesh, the kind used for reinforcing concrete.

Trees and shrubs

❖ Do not **plant your trees** or shrubs too deeply; they tend to settle in, so plant them a little above soil level, form a well around them with soil and mulch. Remember to water new plantings when there is less than an inch of rain in a given week.

❖ If you must plant **single trees** or shrubs in your lawn, surround them with a generous mulched area or ground cover so you don't have to mow near them. Many a plant has succumbed to Lawnmower Blight—a fatal disease, closely related to Bulldozer Wilt and Basketball Decline.

Wildlife and other pests

❖ If you use a hav-a-heart trap to rid yourself of a **groundhog,** be aware that you must take it more than a mile away to prevent it returning. Taking it to another animal's territory may not be the kindest thing, you might consider a more permanent means of dispatch.

❖ **Deer protection**—make it bigger and stronger than you think you need. Protect skinny young trees with caging in August, before rutting season.

There are plants listed as being things that deer will not eat but deer will eat any plant when they are hungry. Protect new plantings: while they may not be something a deer would eat, they are curious and can inflict quite a bit of damage in their wonderment over a new addition to the garden.

❖ Irish Spring Soap has been found to deter deer. Put a portion of a soap bar in a little sack made from old pantyhose, and hang it at deer nose level in the lower branches of trees or in shrubs around the area you wish to protect.

❖ The truth about Cats. They seem to think that the world is their litter box and are particularly grateful when a gardener tills up the ground for them. Place twigs over newly seeded areas or when you plant seedlings. Open flats of seeds or seedlings look a lot like a litter box or a nice place to nap, so cover them with netting. Large pot plants can be protected by putting smaller plants around the soil surface. Cats don't like the smell of citrus, so scatter lemon peel or spray the area with a citrus extract like diluted CitruSolve.

❖ The truth about Dogs. Outside of a dog, man has no better friend. Inside of a dog it is very dark.

Winter

❖ **Frost.** Unless you are willing to go to unusual lengths, don't bother trying to plant out tender plants before the accepted frost free day in your area. The plants might survive, but they will have been stunted, and plants planted out two weeks later will develop at the same rate with less risk.

❖ Many plants provide **winter interest** for areas where winter is a sad and dour time. Grasses, sedums, rudbeckia have good texture, so don't cut them back in fall. The colorful bark of Stewartia, Korean Dogwood, Black River Birch and Red Twig Dogwood can really be noticed at this time.

❖ The best **protection** a plant can have for winter is to have had good growing conditions in spring and summer.

❖ Northern gardeners can extend their growing season with **cold frames.** Plant lettuce in October. Rouge d'Hiver and Red Oak Leaf are especially cold hardy.

❖ It's a rewarding challenge to try to **overwinter your pelargoniums** (aka geraniums). Keep them in a cool place and only water them to stop them from completely drying out. However, they can harbor a virus and will gradually decline and flower less. Support your local grower and buy disease-free plants each spring.

Extra Tips

Air Freshening Plants

❖ There are a number of houseplants that are particularly suited for purifying the air in your home. These plants produce oxygen and moisture, and filter out toxins in your home or office. Moreover, these plants are known for their ease of growth and maintenance. Some of the best air purifying plants are: lady palm, bamboo palm, rubber plants, dracaena, English ivy, Boston fern, peace lily, corn plant, dragon tree, weeping fig, schefflera, snake plant, king of hearts, prayer plant, oak leaf ivy, spider plant, croton and the peacock plant.

Herbs

❖ The best herbs for indoor cultivation are basil, lemon verbena, rosemary, parsley, sweet marjoram, tarragon and dittany of Crete (*Origamun dictamnus*). Peppermint may also do well in cool, sunny rooms.

❖ If you want to dress up your flower garden, herbs can provide distinctive colors and foliage—and some interesting side effects. Try lavender, gray artemisias, hyssop, bee balm, calendula, thyme, sage, rosemary or rue. Rue (*ruta gravedens*), for example, when planted near roses and among vegetables, will ward off Japanese beetles. Cats tend to avoid it—and a rue "tea" sprayed on favorite furniture will discourage scratching.

Unfortunately, rue will also beat up some other herbs—like basil—so be prepared to referee.

❖ Lavender, dill, sage, santolina, geraniums and artemisias do well in pots outdoors.

❖ In or out, most herbs prefer ordinary, well-drained garden soil; members of the mint family will do better in fairly rich, moist soil.

❖ Most herbs should be harvested in the morning, when the plants' oils are most concentrated.

❖ Herbs will grow in almost any kind of container as long as it drains well, either with a hole in the bottom or a layer of material to keep the roots above extra water: dry cinders, gravel or packing peanuts.

❖ The Herb Society of America, 300 Massachusetts Ave, Boston, MA 02115, is a good source of information.

❖ Always brew herbal teas and infusions in clay, china or porcelain teapots. Metal pots can affect the chemistry of the brew.

Vegetables

❖ Strategic plantings of crown imperials (*fritillaria imperialis*) in the vegetable garden will discourage mice, squirrels and other rodents from any bed in which they are growing. Its skunky smell is pervasive—it is strictly for outdoors.

- Grow a bit of rhubarb. The leaves are poisonous: boil them and use a 50% diluted solution as a soil and vegetable anti-pest spray. It also discourages black spot and green fly on roses.

- Make a bit of room in the garden for pyrethrum (*Chrysanthemum coccineum*). Growing live, it helps other plants fight off ticks; the dried flowers can be spread around as an insecticide. It's an ingredient in many insecticide dusts and sprays.

- Plant mustard to attract insects away from your crops. Remove and destroy plants as they become infested.

- Never underestimate the power of mulch. It helps keep the soil moist and cool in the summer, cuts down on watering, discourages weeds, and nourishes the plant beds as it breaks down. Anything you have will serve the purpose—just remember to leave grass clippings on the compost pile for a year or so before you use them if you've been using weedkillers or "weed and feed" fertilizers on the lawn. Use your imagination: if it can break down, it can be used as mulch—pine needles, hay, leaves, newspapers, sawdust, shredded bark, even growing clover!

- The kinds of weeds you get can give you clues to the state of your soil. Acid soil encourages such things as daisies and docks, and pink flowers on chicory. Chicory itself is an indicator of high lime content. Alkaline soil has mustard, thistles and chamomile. Heavy clay will have chicory, coltsfoot and dandelion. Low nitrogen supports clover and vetch. As you amend your soil, you help get rid of weeds!

❖ Soak the contents of ashtrays (butts and ashes) overnight, strain and spray as a pesticide. Gross, but effective. DO wash vegetables well before eating.

Water

❖ Many household water softeners work by taking calcium out of the water and substituting sodium—fine for people, but bad for plants. Sodium makes soil sticky, and it can even be toxic to some plants. A simple solution is to add about ½ teaspoon of gypsum (calcium sulfate) to each gallon of softened water before watering.

❖ Waste not, want not: after it cools, use water from cooking vegetables to water houseplants; keep a bucket in the shower, except when shampooing, to capture "bounce off"; rain butts below your downspouts are back in fashion; soaker hoses are kinder to your plants than sprinklers—more water gets to the roots and less dirt is kicked up.

Final words from "The Black Thumb"

❖ Don't buck Mother Nature. Unless you are prepared to remake your climate, choose plants suited to your ecosystem. You'll save yourself—and the plants—a lot of frustration. Also, living indoors is hard for plants, even at the best of times—there's little sunshine or fresh air, there's high temperatures and low humidity—so if they get sick, they'll probably stay that way. Let them go—it's kinder.

- ❖ Know thyself. If you live to garden, go for the glory! However, if your attention span is short, stick to quick-return vegetables instead of long-term crops, and annuals instead of bulbs and perennials. There's little sadder than a garden abandoned due to lack of interest. Conversely, there is little more soothing to the soul than a well-tended "bit of green" that's all your own.

Happy gardening!

Glossary

boot fairs—swap meets

British Standards Association—British equivalent of FDA and Agriculture inspectors

coir—coconut husks

concertina—accordian

cotton bud—cotton swab

cotton reel—sewing thread spool

dustbin—trash can

jabs—shots

Jeyes fluid—British brand name tar-oil liquid disinfectant cleaner

lash out—splurge

liquidambar—tree whose Asian variety is known as balsam, and whose U.S./Mexican variety is the sweet gum

scree—accumulation of small and broken stones

skep—straw beehive

treacle—molasses

tufa—porous limestone

tussie mussie—decorative dried nosegay

Index

A

A. dracunculoides. *See* Tarragon, Russian
A. kolomikta 69
Acer. *See* Maples
Acer pensylvanicum. *See* Snake bark maple
Achillea 56, 152
Acid soil 3, 198, 229
Acid-loving plants 3
Acidanthera 21
Aconite 44
Actinidia 34, 64
   deliciosa syn. chinensis. *See* Kiwi fruits
   kolomikta 69
Advice 220
Aegopodium podogaria
   'Variegata'. *See* Variegated ground elder
African violet 96, 100
Agastache foeniculum. *See* Anise hyssop
Ageratum 5, 9
Air freshening plants 227
Air plants 97
Ajuga reptens 83. *See* Bugle
Alchemilla 63
   mollis. *See* Lady's mantle
Algae 127
   bottle gardens and terraria 20
Alkaline soil 29-31, 31, 229
Alkanet 180
Allergic skin reactions 86
Allium 21, 22, 26
   christophii 24
   edible 113-115

gigantium. *See* Lilac pompons
tuberosum. *See* Garlic chive
Almonds 112
Aloysia triphylla. *See* Lemon verbena
Alpine plants 3, 138
   chalky soil and 30
Alpine strawberry 167
Alstromeria 13, 21, 156
Alum 56
Alyssum 3, 5
Amaryllis lilies 98
Amelancier canadensis. *See* Shadberry
American red mulberry 69
Anchusa offcinalis. *See* Alkanet
Anemone 3, 159
Angelica 31
Angels trumpets 60, 151
Anise hyssop 180
Annual flowers 5-6
Antirrhinum 5, 9, 152
Ants 79, 123
Aphids 121, 123, 218
Apple
   drying 165
   storing 164
   thinning 171
   trees 140
Aquilegia 3, 159
Arabis 3
Arbour, scented 36
Arches 183-184
Arctic raspberry 68
Artemisia 63
   dracunculus. *See* Tarragon, French
Artemisias 227, 228
Asparagus 10, 153
   as foliage 64
   bigger stalks 185
   officinalis 64
Asperula inctoria. *See* Dyers woodruff

235

Aspidistra 96
Aster 152
Asthma 48
Astilbe 159
Aubergines 185
Aubretia 30, 82, 152
Aucuba 64
   japonica. See Spotted laurel
Autumn colour 6
Avender 180
Aviary 18
Avocado 197
Azalea 3
   bonsai 18

B

Baby blue eyes 179
Back strain 86
Bamboo 13, 31, 64, 146, 159
   handling 146
Bamboo palm 227
Banana skins 145
Barbecue 72
Basal cuttings 136
Basal rotting 28
Basil 77, 92, 94, 227
   storing leaves 165
Bats 196
Bean 8–9, 37, 118
   blackfly and 121
   celery and 40
   chalky soil 30
   dwarf and corn 169
   fertiliser 63
   hanging basket 85
   onions and 40
   sprouts 149
   storing 165
   sweet corn and 40
Bearberry 3
Bearded irises 13
Bedding plants 28
Beds 9–15

Bee balm 227
Beech 87, 106
Beech leaves 57
Bees and wasps 87
Beetroot 10, 149
   storing 165
Begonia 9, 21, 44, 96, 196
Bellis perennis. See Double
   daisies
Berberis 31, 87
Bergenia 82, 83
Berry-bearing trees 17
Betula emanii. See Erman's
   birch
Biennials 12
Birch 30, 182
   Black River 223
   Erman's 198
Birds 15, 17
   bath 15
   feeding 16, 18
   nest 91
   pests 123
Bishop's hat 63
Black mulberry 69
Black River Birch 223
Black spot 146, 229
Black-eyed Susan 6
Blackberry 68, 198
Blackcurrant 66
Blackfly 40, 121
Bladder campion 61
Blanket weed 127
Blue tits 17, 18, 123
Blueberry 3
Bones, compost and 43
Bonfire 146, 193
Bonsai 18–19, 21
Borage 40, 58, 180
Borago officinalis. See Borage
Borax 56
Borders 9–15, 74
   cleaning up 14
Boston fern 227

Botrytis 166
Bottle gardens 19–21
Box 87, 106, 178
   cuttings 139
Boysenberry 68
Bracken 111
Bronze fennel 13
Broom 4, 31, 150, 152, 162
Brugmansia comigera. *See*
   Angels trumpets
Brussels sprouts 81, 118, 197
Buddleia 31, 195
Budgerigars 18
Bugle 63, 64, 82, 83
Bulbs 21–26, 27, 83, 160
   spring 12, 14
   summer 26
Bullace plums 113
Bumblebees 195
Burning bush 14
Butterflies 195
Buying plants 26–28, 27

C

C. maxima. *See* Filbert
C. reticulata. *See* Mandarin
   orange
Cabbage 81
   Jersey Giant 199
   ornamental 7
   root, flies 82
Cacti 28–29, 29
Calamondin orange 69
Calceolaria 9, 96
Calendula 5, 56, 227. *See also*
   Pot marigolds
California poppy 49, 205
Camassia 22, 26
   leichtlinii 22
   quamash 26
Camellia 3, 138
Campanula 3, 9, 179
Candelabra primulas 14, 159

Canna lily 137
   substitute 10
Cape primrose 98
Caper spurge 194
Cardoon 64, 117
Carnation 10, 11, 48, 136
   rooting 50
Carrot fly 142, 144
Carrot 111, 117, 142, 143,
   144, 208
   foliage 117
   frost and 111
   onions and 40
   carrot fly 142, 144
   foliage 143
Castanea sativa. *See* Chestnut
Castor oil 99
Castor oil plant 57
Caterpillars, hairy 87
Catnip 125
Cats 32, 124, 125, 222
   droppings, and compost 43
Celery
   beans and 40
   leaf 185
Celosia 196
Centaurea 5, 63
Cercis siliquastrum. *See* Judas
   tree
Cestrum nocturnum. *See* Night
   jessamine
Chaenomeles. *See* Japonica
Chain-link fencing 61
Chalky soil 29–31
Chamomile 93, 95
Chard 10
Cherimoya 97
Cherries 182
Chestnut 113
Chickweed 191
Chicory 148, 229
Children in the garden 31–32
Chilean flame flower 3
Chilli peppers, storing 165

Chimonanthus praecox. *See*
    Winter sweet
Chinese cabbage 148
Chionodoxa 21
Chive flowers 58
Choisya ternata. *See* Mexican
    orange
Christmas cacti 29
Christmas tree 182
Chrysanthemum 32–33, 136,
    208–209
    coccineum. *See* Pyrethrum
    thinning 172
Cineraria 96
    senecio. *See* Dusty Miller
Cistus 199
Citronella oil 193
Citrus
    mitis. *See* Calamondin orange
    reticulata 69
Clarkia 5, 56
Clary sage 93
Clay soil 33–34, 35
Claytonia. *See* Miner's lettuce
Clematis 34, 35, 36, 38, 49,
    56, 82
    chalky soil and 30
    arbour 36
    planting 38
    slugs and 38
    time to mature 35
Cleome 205
Climbing plants 34–39
Climbing roses 36, 140, 184
Clivia 96
Clock, flowering 198
Clove pinks 59
Clubroot 80, 81
Cob-nut bushes 160
Coco shells 111
Coconut palm 97
Coconut shells 16
Codling moths 123
Coffee grounds 142

Coir compost 133
Colchicums 7
Cold frame 223
    homemade 79
Coleus 9, 64, 96
Colour schemes 39, 63
Companion planting 40–41
Compost 55
    blocker 133
    bonsai 18
    making 41–43
    materials for 229
    recipe for 163
    shredder 147
Composts 132–133
Conservatory 151
Container growing 43–47
    bulbs 21
    buying plants 27
    herbs 228
    transplanting plants 13
Containers 27, 69
Cordon 118
Cordon apples 68
Coreopsis 136, 152
Coriander 95
Corkscrew hazel 198
Corn plant 227
Cornus 64, 82
    alba 'Sibirica'. *See* Dogwood,
    red-stemmed
Corydalis 4, 179
    avellana contorta. *See* Hazel
    bushes
Corylus
    avellana. *See* Hazelnut
    'Contorta'. *See* Corkscrew
    hazel
    x colurna. *See* Trazelnut
    maxima 113
Cosmos 5, 9, 205, 208
    astrosanguineus 151
Cotinus 63
    coggygria. *See* Smoke bush

Cotoneaster 17, 31, 82
Cotton lavender 93
Couch grass and tomatoes 191
Courgette 118, 186
Crab-apple 106, 112
Crane-fly larva 102
Crataegus monogyna. *See*
  Hawthorn
Creeping mints 93
Creeping thyme 30, 101
Creosote 61
Cress 59
Crocus 21, 84, 182
Crop frame 184
Croton 227
Crown imperials 21, 138, 228
Cucumbers 149, 186
Cupressus 63
Curly-leaved parsley 10
Currants 67
  freezing 67
Cut flowers 47–50
Cuttings 50–51, 135, 136,
    138, 145
  camellia 138
  rose 145
Cyclamen 96, 159
Cymbidium 116
Cynara cardunculus. *See*
  Cardoon
Cypress 63, 87

D

Daffodil 21, 25, 26, 49, 84
Dahlia 9, 51–52
  drying 56
  thinning 172
  propagating 135, 136
Daisy 9, 59, 196
Damp places 11
Damson 68, 113
Daphne 4, 31, 150, 151
  rooting 51

Date 97
Datura cornigera syn.
  Brugmansia knightii. *See*
  Angels' trumpets
Day lily 11, 59, 106
Dead nettle 64, 82, 159
Deadhead 45
  bulbs 23
Decorative gourds 48
Deer 194, 221, 222
Delphinium 48, 49, 136
Design 52–54, 206, 209–210
  window-boxes 196, 197
Dianthus 9
  caryophyllus. *See* Clove pinks
Dictamnus albus. *See* Burning
  bush; Gas plant
Dieffenbachia 96
Digging 54–55, 57
Dill 228
Dimorphotheca 152
Dittany of Crete 227
Dividing, ornamental grasses 76
Dogs 123, 124, 222
  droppings, and compost 43
Dogs tooth violets 22
Dogwood 106
  red-stemmed 198
Double daisies 179
Dracaena 96, 227
Dragon tree 227
Dragonflies 130
Dried flowers 210–211
Driftwood, bonsai 19
Drought 189
Dry conditions 14
Dry flowers 55–57, 59
Drying fruit 165
Dusty Miller 206
Dwarf conifers 44
Dwarf willow 4
Dye-plants 180
Dyers broom 180
Dyers woodruff 180

E

E. coccifera. *See* Mount
 Wellington eucalyptus
Earwigs 52, 122
Eau-de-Cologne mint 150
Eccremocarpus 34
Edible flowers 57–59
Edible tubers 36
Eggshells 59–60
Elder 63, 113, 160
 flowers 58
Eleagnus 64, 87
Endive 148
English ivy 227
Epsom salts 63, 104
Equipment 174–178
Eranthus ravannae 220
Eremurus elwesii 23. *See also*
 Foxtail lily
Erman's birch 198
Eryngium 152
Erythronium denscanis. *See*
 Dogs tooth violets
Escallonia 87
Eschscholtzia californica. *See*
 California poppies
Eucalyptus 63
 coccifera 198
 Mount Wellington 198
Eucomis comosa. *See* Pineapple
 flowers
Eucryphia 3
Euonymus 64
 europaeus. *See* Spindleberry
Euphorbia 63, 152. *See also*
 Spurges
 lathyrus. *See* Caper spurge
Evening gardens 60–61 211
Evening primrose 60, 195
Evening-scented flowers 196
Evergreens 106

F

Fairy rings 104
Family garden 32
Fatsia japonica. *See* Castor oil
 plant
Fences 61–62, 63
 wind protection 197
Fennel 93
Ferns 57, 99, 159, 200
Fertilizer 62–63, 148, 207
 bonsai 18
 containers 45
 fuchsias 71
 homemade 62
 houseplants 214
 lawn 216
 pelargoniums 74
Fescue 76
Festuca ovina 'Blueglow'. *See*
 Fescue
Feverfew 40
Ficus 96
Figs 66, 187
Filbert 113
Firethorn 7, 105
Fish 127, 128, 129
Floral preservative 209
Flowering clock 198
Flowering currants 159
Flowers
 edible 57–59
 annual 5, 143
Foeniculum vulgare
 'Purpurescens'. *See* Bronze
 fennel
Foliage 63–64, 65
Forget-me-not 22, 56, 152
Forsythia 87, 152
Fountains 129, 130
Foxes 194
Foxglove 11, 159
 'tea' 49
Foxtail lily 23

Freesia 21, 26, 150
French lavender 14
French marigold, cabbages 40
French pruning 140
French tarragon 95
Fritillaria
  imperialis. See Crown
    imperials
  meleagris. See Fritillary
Fritillary 21, 22
Frost 65
Fruit 65–69
  plants from 97
  storing 164–166
Fuchsia 59, 70–71, 87, 159
  rooting 51
Furniture 71–72

G

Garden, public viewing of 115–116
Gardeners garters 13
Gardenia 96, 150
Garlic 115
  chive 95, 96
  roses and 40
  tea 121
Garrya elliptica. See Tassel
  bush
Gas plant 211
Gates 72–73
Gazanias 199
Genista
  aetnensis. See Mount Etna
    broom
  tinctoria. See Dyers broom
Gentian 3, 4
Gentiana acaulis 138
Geranium 74–75, 206, 228
  in cottage garden 179
  in window-boxes 196
  overwintering 223
Germination 132, 156

Gifts 75
Gladiolus 21, 26, 59, 138
Globe artichokes 56, 57
Glory of the snow 3
Glycerine 57
Godetia 5
Golden conifer 35
Golden hop 37
Golden lonicera 35
Golden privet 35
Gooseberries 65, 67
  thinning 172
Grape hyacinth 21, 22, 84
Grape vine 6, 34, 67
Grapes 67, 187
  thinning 171
Grass cuttings, as mulch 111
Grasses 75–76, 211–212
  winter and 223
Green ethics 77
Green fly 229
Green manure 80
Green vegetables 81–82
Greenhouses 77–80, 151
Grey mould 166
Ground cover 82–83
Groundhog 221
Groundsel 192
Gypsophila 5, 56

H

H. orientalis. See Hellebore
Hamamelis mollis. See Witch
  hazel
Hanging basket 21, 33, 46, 83–85, 132, 188
  cacti and succulents 29
  chrysanthemums 33
  fuchsias 71
  hostas in 46
  tulips in 21
  watering 188
Hardy geranium 4, 82, 152

Hawkmoth caterpillars 195
Hawthorn 87, 106, 178
  birds and 17
  chalky soil and 30
Hazel 112, 184
  bushes 160
  corkscrew 198
  nut 113
Health 85–87, 212
Heather 3, 6, 198
  chalky soil and 29
  foliage 63
  increasing 137
  under planting 163
  winter display 44
Hebe 64, 152, 153
Hedera. See Ivy
Hedge 87, 91, 106
  fruit and nut 112
Heeling-in bulbs 23
Helianthemum 82, 199
Helichrysum 5, 56
Hellebore 22, 48, 56, 138, 159
Helleborus orientalis 22
Helxine soleirolli. See Mind-your-own-business
Hemerocallis. See Day lilies
Herb Society of America 228
Herb tea 213
Herbaceous perennials 135
Herbs 31, 92–96, 212–213, 227–228
  container growing 228
Heuchera 159
Hibiscus 31
Hippeastrum 96. See also Amaryllis lilies
Holly 17, 90, 106, 181, 182
  shaping 178
Hollyhocks 59
Honeysuckle 34, 38, 150
  arbour 36
  chalky soil and 30
  moths and 195

supports 37
Hops 89
  golden 37
  supports 37
Hormone rooting powder 50
Hornbeam 87
Horse chestnut 30
Horseradish 143
Hose 188, 190
  repairing 177
Hosta 14, 64, 82, 83
  hanging basket 46
  propagating 136
  shady area and 159
  white spring display 22
House-leeks 200
Houseplants 96–101
  pests 121, 217
  propagating 97
Humulus lupulus 'Aureus'. See Golden hop
Hyacinth 21, 22, 23, 150
  growing indoors 97
  propagating 138
Hydrangea 56, 152, 159
  blue flowers from 162
  petiolaris 37
Hypericum 82, 87, 106, 152, 159
Hyssop 57, 227

I

Iberis 4, 152
Ice 127
Ice-cream, rose flavoured 58
Ilex 64, 87, 152
Impatiens 5, 9
Insect eaters 17
Insecticide 122, 148, 218, 229
Insects 213
Ipomoea
  bona-nox. See Moonflower
  spp.. See Morning glory

Iris 24, 64
  kaempferi 11
  siberica 11, 106
Ivy 34, 64, 83, 96
  chalky soil and 30
  preserving 57
  variegated 44
  walls and 159, 187

J

J. officinale. *See* Summer jasmine
Japanese beetle 227
Japanese garden, miniature 21
Japanese maple 7
Japanese wineberry 68
Japonica 31
Jasmine 34, 98, 150
Jasminum nudiflorum. *See* Winter jasmine
Jasminum officinale 60
Jersey lily 24
Jerusalem artichokes 143
Joseph Rock 7
Judas tree 30
Juniper 4, 63, 82, 152
  bonzai 18

K

Kale, ornamental 7
King of hearts 227
Kingcup 3
Kiwi fruits 69
Knee 85, 86
Kniphofia 14, 152
Korean dogwood 223
Korean mulberry 69

L

Labelling 215
Laburnum 30, 87, 184, 187
  tree 182

Lady palm 227
Lady's mantle 12, 179
Lamb's lettuce 148
Larch 6
Larkspur 5, 49
Lavender 150, 151, 152
  ants and 123
  encouraging 96
  foliage 227
  hedge 93
  pots 228
Lavendula
  officinalis. *See* Lavender
  stoechas. *See* French lavender
Lawns 101–104
Leaf-mould 42
Leather, compost and 41
Leather-jackets 102
Leeks 111, 114
  flowers 24
  seed heads 57
Lemon balm 180, 213
Lemon verbena 151, 227
Lettuce 148, 149, 223
  thinning 172
Lewisia cotyledon 138
Lighting 120, 128
  house plants 219
Ligularia 83
Lilac 31, 150
  pompons 24
Lilium regale. *See* Regal lily
Lily 22, 26, 138, 150, 159
  Jersey 24
Lily flowers 151
Lily of the valley 22, 48, 101, 152, 159
Limnanthes douglasii. *See* Poached egg plant
Linaria 5, 152
Liquid feed, homemade 63
Liquidambar 6
Lizards 194

243

Lobelia 5, 44, 83, 155, 196
Loganberries 68
Lonicera 87, 178
Loofahs 199
Lovage 31
Love potions 199
Lupins 12, 106, 136
Lyme disease 212

M

M. alba. See White mullberry
M. autralis. See Korean mulberry
M. rubra. See American red mulberry
Maggots 68
Magnolia 31
   stellata 151
Mahonia 82, 159
Mandarin orange 69
Mango 97
Manure 43, 63
   green 80
   hedges and 88
Maple 6, 30, 106, 152
Marestail 192
Marguerite 44, 196
   rooting 51
Marigold 32, 206
Marjoram 57
Marrow
   bush 185
   seeds 123
   storing 165
Marvel of Peru 199
Matthiolis bicorna. See Night scented stock
Mealy bugs 29, 218
Meat, compost and 43
Medlar 106
Melissa officinalis. See Lemon balm
Melon, thinning 171

Mentha spicata 'Moroccan'. See Moroccan mint
Methylated spirits 29
Mexican orange 105
Meyers lemon 69
Micafil 132
Mice 9
Michaelmas daisies 7, 56, 195
   splitting 10
Microwave oven 55
Mildew 67
Mind-your-own-business 99
Miner's lettuce 148
Miniature dianthus 30
Miniature herb garden 94
Miniature rock garden 163
Miniature roses 145
Minimum maintenance gardens 105
Mint 64, 92, 94
   mosquitos and 122
   soil for 228
Mirabilis jalapa. See Marvel of Peru
Miscanthus 64
   sinensis. See Zebra grass
Mizuna greens 148
Mock orange 31, 150
Moles 193, 194
Money from your garden 106–110
Monstera 96
   deliciosa. See Swiss cheese plant
Montia perfoliata. See Miner's lettuce
Moon vine 211
Moonflower 151
Morning glory 37
Morus
   alba 69
   autralis 69
   nigra. See Black mulberry
   rubra 69

Mosquito 122, 128, 193
Moss 200, 215
Mother-of-thousands 99
Moths 195
Mount Etna broom 162
Mount Wellington eucalyptus 198
Mountain ash 30
Mousetrap bait 123
Mower 146, 147
Mulberries 69
Mulberry tree 69
Mulch 102, 110–111, 143, 216–217
  ingredients for 229
Mustard 59, 229
Myosotis 9
Myrtis communis. See Myrtle
Myrtle 151

N

Narcissus 21, 22, 49, 97, 150
Nasturtium 5, 6, 49, 121
  blackfly and 40
  climbing plant 34, 35
  food 58
  tuberous 36
  window-box 196
Nemesia 5, 10
Nemophila menziesii. See Baby blue eyes
Nerine 7
  bowdenii. See Jersey lily
Nests 15, 16, 17
Net orange bags 23
New Zealand flax 64
Newspapers 111
Nicotiana 5, 10, 150
  border 159
  evening garden 60
  moths 195
Nigella 22, 56
Night jessamine 151

Night-scented stock 60, 195, 196
Noise 111–112
Non-diet cola 63
Norway spruce 182
November Pink 7
Nuts 112–113, 113

O

Oak leaf ivy 227
Oak rash 212
Oasis 132
  rooting and 50
Oenothera. See Evening primrose
Old-fashioned roses 145
Onion 113, 115, 117, 142
  beans and 40
  carrots and 40
  flies 40
  storing 165
Orchid 116–117, 117, 151
Organic mulch 111
Oriental brassicas 148
Origamun dictamnus. See Dittany of Crete
Ornamental kitchen garden 117–119
Oxalis 82, 159

P

Pachysandra 82
Painted Lady 37
Pak choi 148
Palms 97
Pampas grass 76
Pansy 21, 44, 59, 84, 196
Parsley 95, 227
Parsnip 111, 142, 157
Pasque flower 4, 137
Passiflora spp.. See Passion flower
Passion flower 34, 35, 37

245

Passion fruit 97
Paths 119–120
  cottage garden and 180
Patio 120–121, 121
  apple tree for 66
  bulbs and 22
Pawpaw 97
Peace lily 227
Peach 187
  growing from stone 65
Peacock plant 227
Peanuts 16
Pear 68
  drying 165
  liqueur 67
  storing 164
  thinning 171
Peas 8–9, 9
Peat 111
Pelargonium 10, 74–75, 196
  See also Geranium
  propagating 136
  window-box 44
Penstemon 10
Peony 48, 56, 106, 217
  moving 13
Peppermint 227
Peppers 185
Perennial
  border 15
  herbaceous 27
  planting 10
  splitting 10
Periwinkle 56, 64, 82, 159
Pesticide, homemade 230
Pests 121–123, 221, 228, 229
  ants 79
  cabbage root flies 82
  crane-fly larva 102
  from bought plants 27
  houseplants 100, 217
  Japanese beetles 227
  leather-jackets 102
  maggots 68

ticks 229
whitefly 40, 77, 81
blackfly 40
cabbages and 41
onion fies 40
Pets 123, 125
Petunia 10
  Purple Wave 206
Phalaris arundinacea. See
  Gardeners garters
Philadelphus 150. See Mock
  orange
Philodendron 96
Phlox 5, 10, 82
Phormium tenax. See New
  Zealand flax
Photographs 125, 127
Picea abies. See Norway spruce
Pieris 159
Pigeons 81
Pineapple
  flowers 26
  mint 150
Pines, bonsai 18
Pinks 5, 15, 82, 150
  in seaside garden 153
  propagating 136
Pittosporum 64
Plants
  buying 26–28, 207
  climbing 34–39
Plastic bags, black and leaf
  mould 42
Plastic flowers 106
Plum, drying 165
Poached egg plant 179
Poinsettia 99, 100
Poison ivy 212
Poisonous plants 87
Polianthes tuberosa. See
  Tuberose
Polyanthus 50, 196
Polygonatum 159
Polygonum 82, 152

Pomegranate 97
Ponds 127–130
Poplar 6
Poppy 5, 56, 198
Pot marigold 40, 59, 180, 196
   See also Marigold
Pot-pourri 131
Potato 30, 34, 142, 143, 144
   storing 165
Potentilla 4, 82, 152
Potting 132–133
Potting mixture, bonsai 18
Powdery mildew 145, 146
Prayer plant 227
Primrose 50, 56
Primula 4, 10, 21, 150, 159
   drying 56
Privet 63, 64, 87, 89, 106
Propagating 135–139
Prostrate juniper 106
Pruning 139–140
Prunus 6
Pulmonaria 82, 83, 159
Pulsatilla vulgaris. *See* Pasque flower
Pump 129
Pumpkin 31
   seeds 123
   storing 165
Pyracantha 17, 34, 88, 152. *See also* Firethorn
Pyrethrins 218
Pyrethrum 229

R

R. arcticus x stellarticus. *See* Arctic raspberry
R. illecebrosus. *See* Strawberry-raspberry
R. phoeniculasius. *See* Japanese wineberry
Rabbits 194
Radish 150, 157, 186, 208

Rainbow bed 39
Rainwater 117
Raised bed 3, 30, 140–141
Rambling roses 140, 184
Ranunculus 56
Raspberries 69
Raspberry beetles 123
Rats 43
Red cabbage 10
Red oak leaf 223
Red twig dogwood 223
Regal lily 150
Removing large trees 141–142
Rhododendron 3, 57, 159
   bonsai 18
   chalky soil and 29
Rhubarb 68, 229
   blanching 68
Ribes. *See* Flowering currants
Ris pallida 'Variegata' 14
Robinia 64
Robins 15, 16
Rock-garden 3, 5, 30
Rocket 148
Rodgersias 64
Roof, tiled; growing plants on 200
Root crops, thinning 172
Root cuttings 135
Root vegetables 142–144, 143
   storing 164
Rooting powder, homemade 74
Rosa
   moyesii 'Geranium' 140
   rubuginosa. *See* Sweetbriar rose
   rugosa 90
   serica pteracantha 144
Rose 31, 34, 88, 144-146, 150, 229
   aphids and 123
   as food 58
   black spot and 229
   buds 56

247

Rose (con't)
  climbing 36
  cuttings 145
  fertiliser and tomatoes 63
  flavoured ice-cream 58
  garlic and 40
  green fly and 229
  hybrid tea 179
  low growing 82
  pruning 140
  suckers 145
  thinning 172
Rosemary 92, 94, 151, 152
  foliage 227
  growing conditions 93
  hedge 88
  topiary 179
Rotavator 55, 146
Rouge d'Hiver 223
Rowan 106, 113, 200
Rubber plant 227
Rubus
  arcticus x stellarticus 68
  cockburnianus. See Blackberries
  illecebrosus 68
  phoeniculasius 68
  spectabilis. See Salmonberry
Rudbeckia 152, 223
Rue 227
Runner beans 37, 183
Ruta gravedens. See Rue

S

S. pratensis. See White campion
Safety 90, 146–148
Saffron substitute 59
Sage 64, 92, 94, 227, 228
Salad crops 148–150
Salmonberry 68
Salsify 149
Salvia 5, 10, 63, 152
  sclarea. See Clary sage

Sambucus nigra. See Elder
Sand pits 32
Sanseveria 96
Santolina 63, 88, 152, 153, 228
  virens. See Cotton lavender
Saponaria 82
Savory 92
Saxifraga 4
Saxifraga sarmentosa. See Mother-of-thousands
Saxifrage 4, 63, 82
Scabiosa 10
Scale 218
Scarecrow 200
Scarlet runner bean 208
Scented
  arbour 36
  flowers 60, 61, 98
  plants 150
  shrubs 151
Schefflera 227
Schlumbergera 96. See Christmas cacti
Scilla 4, 56
Scorzonera 149
Scrophularia 64
Sea holly 153
Seakale 153
Seaside gardens 152–153
Seaweed 42
Sedum 7, 63, 64, 82, 195
  winter and 223
Seed 153–158
  pots 59
  sprouter 149
Semi-shaded borders 159
Sempervivum 4, 63, 152
Senecio 152, 153
  ceucostachys 12
Shadberry 181
Shady area 159–160
Shallot 113, 114
Sheds 161–162
Shredded bark 111

Shrubs 105, 162–163, 221
  chalky soil and 30
  winter colour 198
Silene
  pratensis 61
  vulgaris. *See* Bladder campion
Silica gel 56
Silver sand 56
Sink gardens 163, 165
Sisyrinchiums 199
Skimmia 151
Sloes 113
Slow-worms 194
Slugs 14, 46, 59, 122
  clematis and 38
Smoke bush 31
Snails 17, 59, 122
Snake bark maple 198
Snake plant 227
Snapdragons 48
Snow 164
Snowberry 17
Snowdrop 21, 22, 44, 56
  transplanting 25
Soil
  acid 29–31, 229
  alkaline 29–31, 229
  clay 33–34, 35, 229
  compacted 54
  testing kit 29
  tests 205
Solanum 34, 35
Solomon's seal 159
Sorbus aucuparia. *See* Mountain ash; Rowan tree
Spent hops 111
Spider mites 219
Spider plant 227
Spinach 148
  thinning 172
Spindleberry 30, 106
Spirea 152
Spotted laurel 31, 44

Spring display 45
  white 22
Spurges 139, 159
Squirrels 16, 23, 112
Stachys 82, 152
Stakes 14, 220
Stephanotis 98, 100, 150
Stepping-stones 34, 104
Steps 119–120
Stewartia 223
Stinging nettles 195
Stipa tenufolia 76
Stock 5, 137, 150, 152
Straw 111
Strawberry 85, 166–168, 169
Strawberry-raspberry 68
Streptocarpus. *See* Cape primrose
Subsoil 54
Succulents 28–29
Suckers, rose 145
Sumach 6
Summer jasmine 60
Sun-clock 102
Sundial 200
Sunflower 17, 122
  giant 197, 200
Support 36, 220
  fruit tree 66
  hyacinth 23
  making 15
  materials for 37, 38, 39
  tomato 173
  climbing plants 38
  tall pot plants 99
Swallows 15, 16
Sweet briar rose 64, 151
Sweet corn 10, 117, 168–170, 197
  beans and 40
Sweet marjoram 227
Sweet pea 5, 6, 150, 170–171
  supports 37
Sweet rocket 150

Sweet William 10, 11, 12, 150, 195
Swiss cheese plant 96
Syringa 88

T

Tagetes 5, 10. See French marigolds
Tall grasses 106
Tamarisk 153. See also Tamarix
Tamarix 88, 152. See also Tamarisk
Tansy 123
Tarragon 227
Tarragon, French 95
Tarragon, Russian 95
Tassel bush 34, 163
Teapots 228
Terraria 19–21
Thinning 171–172
Thrift 153
Thrush 17
Thuja 64, 88
Thunbergia alata. See Black-eyed Susan
Thyme 4, 64, 82, 94, 213
  dried flower 57
  growing conditions 93
  lawn 101
Thymus serpyllum 101. See Creeping thyme
Tiarella 82
Ticks 229
Tits 16
Tomato 30, 85, 149, 172–174, 221
  couch grass and 191
  fertiliser and roses 63
  ripening 164
Tongues of fire 37
Tools 91, 139, 146, 147, 174–178

bottle gardens and terraria 20
claims for 205
digging 55
Topiary 178–179
Toxocariasis 43
Tradescantia 96
Transplant pots
  homemade 177
Trazelnut 113
Trees 105, 180–183, 221
  berry-bearing 17
  chalky soil and 30
  climber and 38
  seaside gardens 152
  Sorbus group 7
  winter color 198
Trellis 36, 179, 183
Trillium 159
Tropaeolum
  majus. See Nasturtium
  speciosum. See Chilean flame flower
  tuberosum 'Ken Aslet'. See Nasturtium: tuberous
Tropical plants, bottle gardens and terraria 20
Tuberose 151
Tuberous begonia 196
Tulip 21, 22, 24, 84, 163
  cut flowers 48
  dried flowers 56
  virus 26
Tulipa kaufmania. See Tulip
Tunnels 183–184
Turf 102, 103
Turkey oak 6

V

Vaccinium 82
Vaccinium corym-bosum. See Blueberry
Valerian 187
Variegated ground elder 47

Vegetable garden, colour design 39
Vegetables 184, 185
  green 81–82
  ornamental 10
  storing 164–166
Venus fly trap 97
Verbena 5, 10, 150
  bonariensis 205
Vermiculite 132
Veronica 4, 82, 152
Viburnum 31, 88, 105, 150, 151
Vine weevil 121
Viola 5, 10, 137, 150, 159
  labradorica. *See* Violet
Violet 56, 58, 88
Virginia creeper 6
Virus, tulips and lilies 26
Voles 194

W

Walking-stick, making 199
Wall 36, 144, 159, 186–187
  frost and 65
  north-facing 37
  wind protection 197
Wallflower 10, 11, 12, 45, 150
Walnuts 112
Wasps 194
Water 230
  bonsai 18
  bottle gardens and terraria 20
  features 127–130
  plants 128
  softeners 230
Waterfall 130
Watering 188–190
  cacti and succulents 28
  houseplants 98, 213, 214
Weed killer 102, 104, 148
  homemade 191
Weeds 190–192, 200
  soil type and 229

Weeping fig 227
Weeping willow 181
White campion 61
White lobelia 196
White mullberry 69
White spring display 22
Whitefly 40, 77, 81, 218
Wild flower gardens 192–193
  meadows 216
Wild thyme 93, 94
Wildlife 207, 221, 223
  in the garden 193–196
Wind protection 197
Window in hedges 88
Window-box 29, 44, 45, 84, 196–197
Winter 222–223
  colour 198
  display 44
  fuchsias and 71
  hedges and 88
Winter aconites 25
Winter jasmine 198
Winter squash, storing 165
Winter sweet 150, 162
Wire netting 23
Wisteria 34, 35, 36
Witch hazel 6, 151
Witches 200
Wood-anemones 56
Woodlice 122
Woodmice 194
Worms 42–43
  casts 133
Wrens 15

Y

Yams 10
Yew 88, 106, 178

Z

Zebra grass 76
Zinnia 5, 10, 56, 198–201